STORIES
IN
UNIFORM

STORIES
IN
UNIFORM

*A Look at the Heroics, Sacrifices,
and Triumphs of Our Soldiers*

The Reader's Digest Association, Inc.

New York, NY / Montreal

A READER'S DIGEST BOOK

Copyright © 2013 The Reader's Digest Association, Inc.

The credits that appear on pages 214–215 are hereby made part of this copyright page.

Illustrations: iStockphoto.com (flag and manuscript images); Getty.com (dog tags).

Library of Congress Cataloging-in-Publication Data
Stories in uniform : a look at the heroics, sacrifices, and triumphs of our soldiers / the editors of Reader's Digest. -- 1st edition.
        pages cm
    ISBN 978-1-62145-063-4 (alk. paper) -- ISBN 978-1-62145-064-1 (epub)
    1. United States--History, Military--20th century--Anecdotes. 2. United States-- History, Military--21st century--Anecdotes. 3. United States--Armed Forces-- Biography--Anecdotes. I. Reader's Digest Association. II. Reader's digest.
    E745.S685 2013
    355.00973--dc23

                            2012044020

We are committed to both the quality of our products and the service we provide to our customers. We value your comments, so please feel free to contact us.

            The Reader's Digest Association, Inc.
            Adult Trade Publishing
            44 South Broadway
            White Plains, NY 10601

For more Reader's Digest products and information, visit our website:
            www.rd.com (in the United States)
            www.readersdigest.ca (in Canada)

Printed in the United States of America

10 9 8 7 6 5 4 3 2 1

Contents

THE BOSNIAN WAR

THE GULF WAR

THE WAR ON TERROR

*I*NTRODUCTION

War affects us all. The violence. The destruction. The death of heroes, and the incredible stories of determination and survival. The fearless men and women who go forth to serve our country and fight for our freedom willingly accept their mission. They are part of an army of thousands, and each has a story to tell.

Reader's Digest has been chronicling the deeply moving and complex saga of America in conflict since World War I, and now we have sifted through these real-life stories to provide you with a retrospective of the most extraordinary tales of camaraderie, sacrifice, and heroics all under one cover. These stories are not about the wonder of our Stealth aircraft, nuclear-powered attack subs, and armored battle tanks; these are stories about people—their motivations, their fears, and their triumphs.

These stories illuminate the multifaceted nature of our military history and offer inspiration to all Americans. The brave men and women profiled here are ordinary people who have achieved extraordinary things: They have mastered fear, challenged adversity, and pushed themselves beyond their own personal limits. Their experiences not only provide us with a unique perspective into their world but also inspire us to imagine the impossible and overcome the unimaginable.

WORLD WAR I

★ ★ ★

Unforgettable
Eddie Rickenbacker

BY LOWELL THOMAS

On February 27, 1941, I delivered my nightly newscast over CBS radio with a heavy heart. For the lead item was that Capt. Eddie Rickenbacker, the famed flier and a good friend of mine, had been critically injured in an airliner crash near Atlanta. The odds seemed stacked against him. Still, I remember thinking: *In any fight for life, you've got to bet on Eddie. He's won so many of them.*

Pinned for hours against the dead body of a steward before rescuers could get to him, Eddie had a crushed pelvis, a smashed hip, a crushed elbow, a broken knee, several broken ribs, and one eyeball was lying on his cheek. "He's more dead than alive," an intern said when he was brought to a hospital.

"Let's take care of the live ones." That intern didn't know Eddie Rickenbacker.

"It's going to be painful," one of the doctors warned. "We can't give you an anesthetic."

"Go ahead," Eddie said grimly. "I can take it."

So, marveling at his courage, they put his eyeball back in its socket and sewed the eyelid shut to keep it there. Then they encased him in a plaster cast from chin to toes.

Eddie's condition worsened, and his wife, Adelaide, and two sons were called to his bedside. But he clung stubbornly to life. He woke up groggily one evening in an oxygen tent, the radio near his bed turned to Walter Winchell. "Flash! Eddie Rickenbacker is dying. He is not expected to live another hour." With that, Eddie stuck his one good arm out of the oxygen tent, grabbed a water pitcher and heaved it at the radio. Both tumbled to the floor, smashed. And then he proceeded to recover, although it took four months of almost constant pain.

Eddie once told me he'd had brushes with death 134 times—in aerial combat, auto races, and accidents. He was flirting with death the first time I saw him. I was a student at Valparaiso College in Indiana and went to the road races at Elgin, Illinois.

Afterward, I sought out Rickenbacker, and was astonished to discover that this daredevil was only a year older than myself. He was tall (six-foot-two) and thin, coated with dust, goggles hanging around his neck. I complimented him on his driving. "It isn't all just shut your eyes and grit your teeth," he said. "You gotta know how to take the turns and baby your engine."

Eddie was born in Columbus, Ohio, one of eight children of a construction worker. The family was poor. "A lot of kids had hand-me-downs from their older brothers," he once told me, "but I had to wear my older *sister's* shoes." He dropped out of seventh grade and went to work at age 13 when his father was killed in an accident. Excited by a ride in the town's first Ford runabout, Eddie got a job in an automobile company by offering to work free as a janitor. Impressed by his eagerness, the head of the company, Lee Frayer, promoted him to mechanic. Eddie proved to be a whiz.

When Frayer drove one of his own cars in the 1906 Vanderbilt Cup races, Eddie rode alongside him as mechanic. Before long, the youngster himself was competing against the best drivers of the time. He entered the famed Indianapolis 500 four times. He set a world record of 134 m.p.h. at Daytona Beach, Florida, in a Blitzen-Benz, and in 1916 won 7 of 13 major races, clearing $60,000. He had numerous wrecks, but seemed to have a charmed life. "My angel's wings were always hovering over me," he said.

Then came World War I. When the United States declared war on Germany, Eddie—having recently had his first plane flight—set his heart on becoming an aviator. Over the age limit for pilot training, and lacking the required college degree, he joined the Army and got to Paris as a staff driver for Col. Billy Mitchell, head of the infant Army Air Corps. Eddie finally pestered Mitchell into transferring him to the flying school at Issoudun, France, as head mechanic. There our paths crossed again; I was covering the war as a correspondent. Eddie had learned to fly and had been commissioned, but because of his mechanical experience was assigned to servicing the planes flown by others. "I don't like it one damned bit," he grumbled.

Shortly, however, Eddie was allowed to join the famous "Hat-in-the-Ring" 94th Aero Pursuit Squadron. This blunt-spoken, grease-stained ex-mechanic soon made believers of his fellow pilots. On one of his first combat missions in April 1918, Eddie shot down a German Pfalz fighter. He brought down four more enemy planes in May, and won the French *Croix de guerre*.

He survived innumerable close calls. In one dogfight, half his propeller was shot off. Another time, the fabric covering his upper right wing ripped off in a dive, and he had to nurse the plane home at treetop level, muttering prayers as bullets zinged around him. Many of his battles were with the famed "Flying Circus" of Manfred von Richthofen, the "Red Baron."

He was made squadron commander. "I want no saluting, no unnecessary deference to rank," he said. "We're going to work together as equals, pilots and mechanics alike, every man doing his job." On his first day as commander he downed two planes to win the Congressional Medal of Honor. And his manner inspired confidence in others. His old friend John Wheeler said that before one mission some of his pilots seemed jittery. "I expect to live to be 90 and then be arrested for rape," Eddie told them. During October, he bagged 14 enemy aircraft, bringing his total to 26. When the war ended, his squadron had shot down 69 German planes, more than any other American unit. And he was the "Ace of Aces."

Eddie came home as one of the country's most acclaimed heroes. Swamped with offers, he chose something he knew—

the automobile business. He liked to say that America's greatest freedom was the freedom to go broke, and he found out the hard way. Backed by a group of financiers, he designed and manufactured a sporty car called the Rickenbacker, which introduced four-wheel brakes. But, unable to buck the big automotive companies, he wound up $250,000 in debt.

It didn't daunt him. "Failure is the greatest word in the English language," he declared. "If you have the determination, you can come back from failure and succeed."

He proved it. He not only paid off his debt but raised $700,000 more to buy the Indianapolis Speedway. There, amid the zoom of speeding cars and the rough camaraderie of the drivers, he was in his element. His parties on the eve of each Memorial Day race raged until dawn, with Eddie presiding by pounding on a table with a baseball bat.

In 1934 General Motors persuaded Eddie to take over Eastern Airlines, a money-losing subsidiary. Within a year the penny-pinching Eddie had it in the black. And when GM decided to sell the airline, Rickenbacker scrounged up $3.5 million and bought it. Captain Eddie, as the employees called him, ran the airline as he had run his fighter squadron, with all-out effort. He did everything from changing tires to selling tickets.

One time Eastern had a rash of passenger complaints about luggage going astray. So when the airline's management personnel came to Miami for a meeting, they were told their baggage would be delivered to their hotel rooms—but Eddie had it locked up overnight. The men turned up for the meeting the next morning unshaved, teeth unbrushed, wearing dirty shirts. "Now you guys know how the customer feels when you mishandle his luggage," declared Rickenbacker.

Despite his rough-and-tumble methods, Eddie had a deep regard for his employees. He installed the first airline 40-hour week, the first pension fund, group insurance and a stock-option plan. He pioneered in hiring war-veteran amputees.

His grasp of detail was amazing. Once, on a visit to Eastern's Miami shops, he found an overhaul crew trying to figure what was wrong with a disassembled engine. Eddie spotted a gear about the size of a saucer that didn't look right. "How many teeth is this thing supposed to have?" he asked. "Forty-five," the crew boss said, checking the blueprint. "Then here's your trouble," said Eddie, handing him the gear. "It's got 46." He was right.

Eddie took time off from his Eastern job only during World War II, when he journeyed the globe to report on the Allied air situation to world leaders. At one point he was asked to deliver a top-secret message to Gen. Douglas MacArthur, then directing the Pacific fighting from Port Moresby, New Guinea. With a crew of seven, Eddie took off from Honolulu on October 21, 1942.

On my newscast the next night, I again had the heart-wrenching task of broadcasting ominous news of Eddie. His plane had failed to reach its first scheduled stop, Canton Island, a speck of land in the vast South Pacific. Days turned into weeks as the Navy continued to search for the missing plane. Despite dwindling hopes, I still had faith in the special destiny of my indestructible friend. Yet I could scarcely believe it myself when the news came chattering over the teleprinter wires that Eddie and six of his seven companions had been rescued, more dead than alive, after floating in three life rafts for 24 days.

Eventually Eddie told me the full story of the incredible ordeal. Their plane missed tiny Canton Island in the darkness, ran out of fuel and had to ditch at sea. Several of the men were hurt in the splashdown, and rations and water were lost in their scramble out of the sinking plane. "All we had were four small oranges," Eddie said. Although he was the only civilian, his tough personality made him the leader. To make the four oranges last, he divided one into eight small parts only every other day.

Roped together, the three rafts bobbed on the ocean swells day after weary day, the men sprawled together, some groaning from their injuries. Eddie, wearing a business suit and an old fedora, sat hunkered down scanning the endless expanse of ocean. Scorched by the tropical sun, and chilled at night by flying spray, all developed running sores. Sharks bumped against the rafts. "Salt water will kill you," Eddie warned. "No matter how thirsty you get, don't touch a drop." After they had been afloat eight days, it rained and Eddie divided up the rain they caught.

When a sea gull landed on his head, Eddie deftly grabbed it and they ate it—a seeming miracle that buoyed their hopes. But as days dragged by, the men neared the end of their endurance. One man died. Abrasively, Eddie taunted the others to stay alive. Some were determined to live, just for the pleasure of seeing him die. Finally a patrolling plane sighted them. Eddie had shrunk from 180 pounds to 126. But he resumed his journey and delivered the message to General MacArthur in person, if a bit late.

After the war, Rickenbacker returned to running Eastern Airlines with his same old vigor. For 25 consecutive years under his direction the airline showed a profit, a record unequaled in that business. At the age of 73 he stepped down, to devote his remaining years to spreading the gospel of patriotism and rugged individualism. Eddie believed emphatically in the old-fashioned virtues: thrift, hard work, love of country, and belief in God. Morning and night, he got down on his knees to pray.

Because he spoke his mind, and had little regard for people who straddled issues or compromised, Eddie struck some people as a crusty curmudgeon. Yet he was a kindly and generous man. Paid $25,000 for his account of his ordeal in the Pacific, he donated the check to the Air Force Aid Society. And he gave his 2700-acre ranch in Texas to the Boy Scouts.

As he grew older, all that his tough body had endured inevitably took its toll. Appropriately, his last public appearance was in a parade in Miami last July 4, when he was 82.

I saw him shortly afterward. His hair was thin and white, and he walked with a cane, but he brushed aside attempts to help. I congratulated him on recovering from a recent critical illness and surgery. "I've cheated the grim reaper more times than anyone I know," he said with a laugh. "That was number 135."

A few days later word came from Switzerland, where he had taken his beloved Adelaide for medical treatment, that Eddie was ill himself. Then in Zurich, not far from the little farms where his parents were born, his great heart was stilled at last.

When I think of him now, inevitably there comes to mind

his favorite Psalm, read at prayer meetings he held on the raft in the Pacific. The words define his deep faith in God and in his own remarkable destiny: "If I take the wings of the morning, and dwell in the uttermost parts of the sea, even there shall thy hand lead me and thy right hand shall hold me."

An excellent writer known for his strong, deep voice and love of far-flung places, Lowell Thomas was one of the very first to enter the field of radio and television broadcasting. Fearless, he brought back eyewitness accounts from the battlefields in World War I and during World War II often reported from a mobile truck behind the front lines. His radio program, Lowell Thomas and the News, *ran for 46 years, the longest in U.S. history.*

WORLD WAR II

★ ★ ★

The Invasion

From Eisenhower's hidden headquarters, tense nerve center of it all;
from the flagship of the mighty armada that performed the miracle
of reaching the coasts of France undetected; from the bloody beach,
shoulder to shoulder with the GIs, three Reader's Digest *correspondents*
eyewitness the unfolding of the tremendous drama of the invasion.

I. The Great Decision

Behind the Scenes with Eisenhower

BY ALLAN A. MICHIE

Roving Editor of The Reader's Digest, *accredited*
to General Eisenhower's headquarters

Four years ago, before the last British soldier was taken off the
beach at Dunkirk, Prime Minister Churchill assigned a small
group of officers to the specific task of planning the return to

the Continent. Then and for a long time afterward, it seemed a mere academic exercise. But by the time of the Casablanca conference in early 1943, the project no longer looked fantastic and the plans for D Day filled four huge volumes, each the size of a New York telephone book.

The place where the invasion would strike was decided over a year ago. Roosevelt, Churchill and the Combined Chiefs of Staff approved the decision in August 1943 at Quebec.

That it would start between the end of May and the middle of June 1944 was decided at least eight months in advance. In November 1943 at Teheran, President Roosevelt so informed Marshal Stalin. The exact day was to be left to Eisenhower. Marshal Stalin expressed his complete satisfaction.

When General Eisenhower arrived in London in January, he checked over the forecasts of the men and equipment he could expect, and on what dates. Satisfied, he set invasion week to be between June 3 and 10.

But the selection of the precise day was a last-minute drama.

Four or five weeks before D Day, SHAEF (Supreme Headquarters Allied Expeditionary Forces) departed from London and moved into battle headquarters conveniently near the loading ports and the "hards"—stretches of English beach paved with blocks onto which landing craft come at high tide.

In a big, stodgy old house that has seen better days, standing in a rolling, wooded private park was the nerve center of the entire invasion operation.

Vital pieces of information poured into this quiet woodland hideout—photographs taken by suicide pilots at zero feet above Normandy beaches showing five main types of mines and underwater obstacles to impede our landings, photographs of vital bridges and railway yards bombed to uselessness. The preparatory air attacks began eight weeks before D Day and by June 6, 82 strategic railway centers behind the Atlantic wall had been put out of action and most rail and road bridges leading to the Cherbourg Peninsula had been broken, forcing Germans to move up supplies and reinforcements by long detours. The air policy was to drop two bombs elsewhere, as on Pas de Calais, to one on the real invasion objective, to divert German suspicion.

A few days before D Day, the Channel clearing plan started working. Allied destroyers and planes, with interlocking sweeps, covered almost every square yard of the English Channel while other forces bottled it up at both ends. U-boats were unable to surface long enough in the area to charge batteries without being detected. German E-boats and R-boats were driven back to bases whose approaches were mined nightly by planes to make impossible any sudden sortie against the invasion fleet. Heavier ships of the Home Fleet cruised through the North Sea approaches ready to intercept any bigger German warships. Intelligence reports, corroborated by photographs, described hidden big gun emplacements on the coast which had not previously been detected.

At the last minute a German sergeant deserted his Führer and at pistol point forced French fishermen to take him to England. He brought with him valuable details of the Atlantic wall defenses along the Normandy coast. But by that time the Atlantic wall had few secrets from us.

The British had long ago issued an appeal for snapshots taken in peacetime by trippers onto the Continent. From the thousands sent in, valuable details were ferreted out—a narrow lane not shown on any maps that led up behind a cliff on which the Germans had installed a heavy gun battery; a back alley that curves behind a tourist hotel which the Germans had made into a strong point.

As far back as March 29 troops began moving into staging areas, then closer to embarkation ports, then finally to their loading areas. Nearly 2000 special troop trains were run to coastal ports. In the great control room an illuminated map showed the progress of every convoy along the roads to the ports. Meanwhile, in large areas of Britain, evacuated by civilians, troops were training with live ammunition. Rommel's beach obstacles were duplicated and demolition squads practiced taking the sting out of them.

As a result of the Dieppe experience, special landing craft fitted with rocket batteries were developed to mow down German beach obstructions. Tens of thousands of vehicles were waterproofed for beach landings and equipped with flexible tubing and steel chimneys that reared high above the engines to suck down air to the motors as they plunged through surf up to the drivers' necks. Some 280 British factories were set working day and night and the entire output of Britain's sheet steel rolling mills was taken over for this great job. The intricate task of loading the invasion ships took two years of expert planning.

The endless ammunition dumps built up along quiet English lanes actually contained more ammunition than was used in all of World War I. Tanks were parked track to track; aircraft stood wing-tip to wing-tip; miles-long convoys of trucks, bulldozers, ducks and self-propelled guns were parked in fields and at roadsides until Britons wondered if their little island would sink under the weight.

Just 30 days before D Day, the last full-scale invasion exercise was completed. Tired GIs and Tommies who had participated in a half-dozen such exercises complained that next time they were called out they wanted to go straight into action. Landing-craft crews who had frequently been sent out on feints to deceive the enemy felt the same. They got their wish.

Seven days before D Day, which was originally set for Monday, June 5, final loading up began.

As the days ticked off, the tension at SHAEF mounted higher and higher, but at the personal headquarters of the commanders there was an atmosphere of calm. Monty [Field Marshal Bernard Montgomery of the British Army] left to subordinates the detail work, which he abhors, and read his favorite author, Anthony Trollope.

Eisenhower refused to move into the big house but set up tent headquarters in the woods. He sleeps in what he calls his "circus wagon," built on a 2½-ton army truck chassis—an idea borrowed from Monty. Its one room is littered with an odd assortment of Wild West yarns and psychological novels.

On Friday afternoon, June 2, Prime Minister Churchill and Field Marshal Smuts dropped into Eisenhower's camp after touring the coast to watch loading operations on the "hards." The three men talked for an hour. Churchill suggested that he should go along with the assault forces on D Day.

General Eisenhower at first passed off the Prime Minister's remark as a joke, but Churchill returned to the point and finally Eisenhower said flatly that Churchill could not go. He reminded the Prime Minister that if he were lost, things would be disorganized in Britain and the whole military operation would be endangered. "Besides," continued Eisenhower, "the warship you'd be on would require more protection than we'd ordinarily give it."

Churchill was persistent. "After all," he said, "I am Minister for National Defense. I can put myself aboard a British warship as an officer. Even the Supreme Commander cannot dictate the complement of a British naval vessel."

While Churchill was speaking in this vein, he was informed that Buckingham Palace was calling him on the telephone. It was the King, who had learned of his Chief Minister's purpose in visiting Eisenhower.

Under no circumstances, said the King, was Mr. Churchill to consider going to France on D Day.

Churchill acceded, in downcast mood.

Saturday evening, June 3, General Eisenhower held the first of four conferences that were to determine D Day, H Hour. The conferees were Monty, neatly dressed for a change, in a new battledress just sent him from the United States; quiet, soft-spoken Air Chief Marshal Sir Arthur Tedder, Eisenhower's brilliant deputy; Allied Naval Commander in Chief, small, peppery Admiral Sir Bertram Ramsay, the man who had brilliantly improvised the "operation dynamo" that rescued the troops from Dunkirk.

Last to arrive was Air Chief Marshal Sir Trafford Leigh-Mallory, Commander of the Allied Expeditionary Air Forces. He had flown down from London in his private puddle-jumper aircraft.

Outside in the fading half light of an English summer day, the weather appeared good to a layman's eyes, but to the weather experts at SHAEF the forecast was discouraging. There were three chief weather midwives assisting at the birth of the great invasion—two British officers and an American Air Force colonel. For weeks past they had been producing forecasts and charts almost hourly. Now their predictions were not favorable. Weather over the Channel and France would worsen steadily, bringing low ceilings which would cancel out air activity, also high winds and rough seas which would hinder beach landings.

Final decision was postponed until 4:30 next morning (Sunday, June 4), and the High Commanders separated to get a few hours' sleep. When they met Sunday morning, the weathermen confirmed their earlier forecasts and it was decided to postpone the invasion at least 24 hours. If the weather continued bad, the whole operation might have to be set back for weeks until the tides and moon again would be right for landings. For only one day in any month would be really suitable. The moon must be full—to let airborne troops operate effectively, to give our fighter-cover and anti-aircraft a chance to keep the Luftwaffe away, and to make difficult the operation of the Nazis' light-shy but very effective E-boats. The tide had to be at low ebb three hours before dawn to expose underwater obstacles for demolition and make the beach right for H-Hour landing.

On Sunday evening, June 4, the Prime Minister and Smuts— later joined by General de Gaulle—dropped in on Eisenhower and sat for a long time discussing aspects of the momentous decision that was Eisenhower's alone to make. They left, and at nine o'clock, Eisenhower held another staff conference at

SHAEF. The weathermen were called in singly. Their forecasts, arrived at independently of each other, tallied and they made a more favorable picture. There was every prospect that weather over France and the Channel would steadily improve during the next 48 hours.

The High Commanders and their Chiefs of Staff weighed the gamble they were about to take. After 45 minutes, tentative agreement was reached that the invasion would go on. But they decided to hold one last conference at 4:30 on Monday morning, June 5, for the final word.

Back at his caravan, General Eisenhower turned in and slept a few hours. At four o'clock, he went back to SHAEF. Around the table sat Tedder, Montgomery, Leigh-Mallory, Admiral Ramsay and their Chiefs of Staff. The first weatherman was called in. He stuck to his original forecast. There was good weather ahead. It might not come for a day or two. On the other hand it might come within 12 hours. The other two weathermen, separately questioned, agreed.

General Eisenhower summed up the position to his Commanders. Everything was ready. If they delayed much longer, German reconnaissance aircraft were bound to find out the extent of mass shipping and landing craft assembled off the ports. The American assault force and the United States naval task force were already under weigh, and the longer they stayed at sea, the more difficult it would be to keep the many landing craft shepherded into convoys. A few more days under German observation and the invasion might lose its chance of tactical surprise.

The weather was a gamble, General Eisenhower admitted,

but it was up to himself and the High Commanders to rise to it, or turn away. They all knew what turning away implied— delay, perhaps of weeks; the intricate loading process to be done over again; bad effect on the morale of troops.

Eisenhower turned to Admiral Ramsay and asked, "What do you think?"

Ramsay replied, "I'd like to hear the 'Air' give his views."

Air Chief Marshal Leigh-Mallory spoke with deliberation but left no doubt that "Air" was willing to gamble on the weather experts' predictions.

"All right," said Admiral Ramsay, with mock belligerency, "if the 'Air' thinks he can do it, the Navy certainly can."

General Eisenhower smiled, but only briefly. This was the moment the peoples of the Allied nations had sweated and toiled for. Looking down the table at his commanders, his face more serious than it ever has been or is likely to be again, he said quietly, "Okay, let 'er rip."

Those around the table rose quickly and hurried from the room to set the operation in motion. Ike called after them, "Good luck!"

He was last to emerge from the room. He was walking heavily, and those who saw him remarked later that each of the eight stars on his shoulders seemed to weigh a ton. He drove quickly back to his "circus wagon" and turned in without waking his aides. . . .

With the mammoth operation at last under way, there was no one more useless than the Supreme Commander. During the long day before D Day, General Eisenhower had nothing to do but visit his troops. In the morning, he drove to a nearby port and chatted with British soldiers loading on their LCI's. In the evening he drove to airfields where men of the 101st U.S. Airborne Division were loading in their transport planes and black gliders. As he rolled up in his four-starred Cadillac at airfield after airfield, the men were already coloring their faces with cocoa and linseed oil. He went about from group to group wisecracking with them, partly to relieve their tension, partly his own.

As the boys climbed into their dark planes, the General called out, "Good luck!" He was noticeably affected. To drop several divisions of airborne and paratroop forces miles behind the Atlantic wall, long before H Hour on the beaches, was a tremendous risk. Many of his own staff officers, British and American, had strongly advised against it. If the beachheads weren't established securely it meant several divisions of superbly trained troops would be lost. The General took the risk. He knew that, in taking it, he was sending some of them to certain death. They knew it, too.

The first phone call on D Day, June 6, came to Eisenhower's office about 7 a.m. Commander Harry Butcher, Eisenhower's friend and naval aide, answered. It was Leigh-Mallory reporting that airborne and paratroop landings had been unbelievably successful and that the first assault landings had been successfully made. Butcher stepped across the cinders to Ike's "circus wagon" expecting to find the General still asleep, but he was in bed propped up behind a Wild West novel. Butcher told him Leigh-Mallory's news. "Am I glad!" breathed the General.

Admiral Ramsay reported that the naval part of the show

was 100 percent successful, with few losses. In fact, the landings had taken the Germans entirely by surprise. Ramsay had craftily sent a decoy convoy up through the Channel late on the eve of D Day. The German coastal gunners had opened up with everything they had on the unfortunate decoy convoy and then shut down for the night. Whereupon the real invasion armada sailed unmolested right to its goal.

At breakfast that D-Day morning, General Eisenhower was animated and happy for the first time in months. He talked to Butcher about other D days he'd been on—North Africa, which he directed from Gibraltar; Pantelleria, Sicily, which he directed from Malta; and Salerno. Compared to these, said the General, the invasion of France had produced the quietest D day of all.

The weather remained his biggest worry, and even before Butcher had called him he had been out of his caravan, peering up at the skies through the trees. As the sun began occasionally to peep through the clouds he relaxed.

At the nerve center of SHAEF there was one chilling moment that morning, when the first signal came from the beaches. It was rushed to the Staff Chiefs. They opened the message and read that the first assault wave had drowned. Faces went white. Then someone asked hurriedly for a repeat on the message. For a minute or two they waited. Then came the repeat. There had been a mistake. The correct message was that the first assault wave had *grounded*.

Within 48 hours of H Hour, the invasion spearhead had established a foothold in France. And without the frightful toll of casualties that professional pessimists had predicted.

On D-plus-six, a week after the invasion began, more than 500 square miles of Europe had been occupied by Allied armies. The battle was by no means over. The lives of many of our bravest and best were yet to be taken. But the bridgehead into France had been established.

What Philip of Spain and Napoleon failed to do, what Hitler never had courage to try, the Allied armies under Eisenhower had dared and done.

II. Armada in Action

The Channel Crossing on the Flagship

BY FREDERIC SONDERN, JR.

Roving Editor of The Reader's Digest, *accredited to the U.S. Navy*

This was it—D Day and almost H Hour. A few miles ahead on the low-lying coast of France, not far from Cherbourg, a lighthouse winked peacefully. The bridge telegraph tinkled and our engines stopped throbbing. The anchor chain rattled through its hawsehole. Our whistle roared a short, hoarse signal and all around us the silhouettes of dozens of other ships came to rest. It was very quiet there in the moonlight; much too quiet, I thought, as we waited for the first German gun to blast its challenge from the shore.

They could hardly believe it in the wardroom of the flagship. Turning from a big wall chart, the Admiral's navigation officer shut his dividers with a snap. "On the nose, by God!" he announced. The intelligence officer rubbed his head. "Not a smell of them all the way across," he said, "and if they knew we were here, they'd have opened up already." The chief of staff smiled his wry smile. "Maybe they're just waiting to give us a surprise when they get us figured out. We can't be *that* good."

But he was wrong. The big German coastal batteries remained silent, and as nerve-racking minutes ticked by, the battleships, transports and landing craft of our task force slid into their exactly prearranged positions unmolested.

It was very quiet in the ship, too. We had been steaming all day on a long zigzag course, designed to make the Germans think us heading for Pas de Calais rather than the Cherbourg Peninsula. Spirits were gay during the morning. The long, dull months of training were over at last, and the colossal spectacle we were watching took our minds off what lay ahead. Troops lined the rails as we picked up unit after unit of our tremendous convoy at various meeting places along the coast. There were endless rows of waddling tank and infantry landing ships— their barrage balloons bobbing crazily in the sky above them— flanked by escort craft of every kind.

And then over the horizon came the impressive line of our supporting warships. A deft maneuver brought us into column ahead of the battleship *Nevada* and the cruisers *Tuscaloosa* and *Quincy*. The big guns bristling behind us looked very good. "Gee," said a young soldier standing next to me, "that's a lot of cannons."

I agreed happily that it certainly was a lot of cannons.

As the afternoon wore on, tension grew. Everybody was being very polite. On the bridge, even the crusty officer who ran the ship gave orders less brusquely than usual. But there were no jitters, no traces of hysteria. A leathery Marine colonel, veteran of many battles, managed a wintry smile and said that, for green troops, the kids looked pretty promising. Coming from him, that was praise indeed.

When an alarm bell suddenly began to clang and a bosun's rasping voice came over the intercom—"All hands man your battle stations!"—the call to general quarters was welcome relief. There really was a Nazi plane ahead this time. It was 10:30 p.m. But nothing happened.

In the combat intelligence room—nerve center of the Admiral's command post—a vast picture of the big crossing was unfolding. We were one of two invasion forces—American, under Rear Admiral Alan Kirk, U.S.N., and British, under Sir Philip Vian, Royal Navy. Five thousand ships were moving across the English Channel, assembled from several dozen ports and routed on exact schedule through narrow lanes swept and marked by minesweepers several hours before. The two task force commanders were linked with each other and with Supreme Headquarters ashore by the most intricate military communications system ever devised.

There was surprisingly little activity, however. The operation plan covered all details of every ship's movements and it worked like a clock.

It was about 1:30 in the morning of June 6 when an officer in the combat intelligence room suddenly barked: "Two hundred planes coming over."

"Enemy?" shrilled a young officer. "No," said the commander, "they'll be the airborne boys."

And they were. One, two, three-, and then score after score of the big transports thundered by overhead. On the peninsula,

German flak began roaring and searchlights swept the sky.

A few minutes later, the commander turned to the radio-man monitoring German military stations, alert for the first sudden burst of activity. "Well?" he asked. We held our breaths. "Still very light traffic, sir," said the British expert, reading a Western thriller as he twiddled his dials. He was very efficient, and he always caught everything worth catching, but he considered the war, as he told me, a very dull way of earning one's living. He wasn't at all disturbed, as I was, about the danger of German searchlights picking us up. Fortunately, when they started poking around, the beams were deflected by clouds, and the Nazis apparently decided it was just another air raid. The coastal batteries, which could have given us terrible punishment, were still silent.

We knew that just then airborne divisions were going down. Parachutists went down first, to clear strategic fields of the poles and other traps which the Germans—forewarned by careless publicity of the scope of our airborne operations—had set for gliders. The parachutists worked quickly with grenades and mine detectors, but the glidermen suffered casualties nevertheless.

Along the beaches, Commandos and Rangers were busy, too. A dozen large units were mopping up crucial strong points, overrunning coastal batteries and wrecking communications centers. One of the most powerful German coast-defense batteries was tucked away in a huge concrete fortress, almost impregnable even to air and artillery attack. Immensely massive steel doors barricaded its entrance. Two Commandos stole a German staff car and, yelling, *"Die Invasion hat begonnen!"* at the top of their lungs, they careened up to the sentries and startled them into opening the gates wide enough to throw in their bombs. After that the gates could not be closed, and within a few minutes the last of the German garrison fell under a hail of lead from the Commandos' tommyguns.

Up and down 60 miles of coast, the preinvasion raiders were doing their work on schedule. Their incredible exploits will make one of the greatest chapters in military history.

All this, however, seemed very far away to us on the Admiral's flagship. As the reports came in, a bell would ring. The commander would read the message and put a new sticker on his chart. Finally, at three o'clock, the silence ahead of us split wide open. Pathfinder planes of the RAF had roared by overhead. Huge chandelier flares, red and green, came down over the beach. And then all hell broke loose. Geysers of fire and sand in closely patterned rows flashed upward as bombers, following their guides, laid down stick after stick. German flak spat from all directions, their tracers arching fantastic fireworks into the sky. They were pretty accurate, and from time to time a mortally wounded plane would plunge blazing earthward like a meteor, ending in a leaping flash of fire as it struck the ground.

On the bridge, a veteran captain—seemingly oblivious of the din—gave orders for lowering landing craft from our davits. He paused to look at the booming, lethal pyrotechnics and remarked to another correspondent and me that they reminded him of a "hell of a Fourth of July" he remembered as a kid.

All around us landing boats were forming circles ready to take off the troops from transports for the dash ashore. "Boat team number five form at station three" came the bosun's bored voice over the loudspeaker system.

Dawn was breaking, and on the flag bridge, the Admiral and the General commanding the division we were putting ashore were worried. The waves were too high and the landing craft were bobbing around like corks. Troops clambering down the nets were having a tough time. Every time a GI landed with a smack on the bottom of his boat—his tin hat flying in one direction, his gun in the other—our hearts went into our throats. Was this going to be the catastrophe we had just avoided in the Sicilian landing?

Somehow at last the landing craft were loaded. The bleak strained faces at command positions began to relax. At 5:40—as though at touch of a button—the warships ahead of us began bellowing. Our teeth rattled as flash followed flash and shells of every caliber whined from the battleships, cruisers and destroyers into the beach. Over the whole assault area, 600 guns in 80 ships put down 2000 tons of explosives in ten minutes.

Actually both the bombing and the naval gunnery were the most carefully prepared and coordinated barrage of the war. On the highly important chart in the wardroom that scheduled the attack of every bomber squadron and the fire of every ship in our task force, German positions and batteries were marked. Their priority for attention had been decided according to their size, range and ability to interfere with our operation. One coastal battery particularly, set in the side of a hill and practically invulnerable to air attack, could have mauled us badly while unloading. "That one, gentlemen," the Admiral had said at pre-D-Day briefing, "is a *must*." Salvos of 14-inch shells from one of our battleships began hitting it precisely on schedule and, when a Ranger party arrived there a little later for mopping up, they found not one live German in the fortification.

Small, slow spotting planes cruised lazily over the target areas, their observers talking directly to their fire-control officers afloat and correcting aim as the shells came over. It was beautiful shooting and at almost regular intervals the commander in our intelligence room put a new sticker against one of the red rings on the chart. "DESTROYED," it said.

Behind this curtain, the loaded landing boats formed exactly spaced waves for the final run to the beach. Heading them, Navy scouts in control craft found the exact boundaries of assigned beaches—no easy job in the dust and smoke of a bombardment which had blasted almost every recognizable landmark, and in the teeth of machine-gun and vicious mortar fire. The scouts guided in demolition crews of the naval beach battalion who, with their bombs and Bangalore torpedoes, had to blast a way through the maze of hedgehog-like steel structures, upended rails, barbed wire and mines. We could see them calmly paddling boats and setting their charges, with lead and steel slapping the water all around them. The leaders of this toughest job were men with Mediterranean experience, but the rest were boys being shot at for the first time.

Through cleared channels came like clockwork the personnel landing craft loaded with troops, and tank landing craft, with tanks firing from them. Over their heads and from the flanks, rocket craft sent fantastic salvos swishing, to explode mines on shore with their closely patterned miniature earthquakes and to tear open barbed wire. Small, fast rocket craft, motor torpedo boats, flak ships and destroyers close inshore poured a last burst of drenching fire, then again as by clockwork the curtain lifted and the leading landing craft rammed their bows into the sand, to drop ramps and discharge line after line of crouching, running, firing men and roaring tanks.

It was H Hour and the invasion had begun.

On and behind some of the beaches in the hours just before and after H, bad luck and mistakes caused heavy losses. One airborne outfit struck an area which the Germans happened to be using for anti-invasion maneuvers. Nazi machine gunners were in place and waiting as the Allied troops stepped out of the gliders. In one beach sector, the landing force struck an accidental last-minute German troop concentration.

The weather was not at all cooperative. Four-foot waves delayed troop loading at some places by over 60 minutes past schedule. By that time, the fast Normandy tide had dropped sharply, landing craft grounded far out and left men wading through four feet of water and under leaden hail without cover. The delay let the Germans regroup their artillery and it cost us lives, but it did not give them time to bring up sizable reinforcements, which might have caused disaster.

On the whole, however, surprise was complete. The picture I had seen ahead of me was repeated on beaches up and down the line. The Germans had, as a gold-braided wit said, been "caught with their panzers down." The American and Royal navies had fulfilled Admiral Ramsay's promise to Eisenhower—"We will land you there to the inch." "The miracle," as Ernie Pyle wrote, "of landing there at all" had been accomplished.

III. Beachhead Panorama

Going Ashore with the Troops

BY IRA WOLFERT

Wolfert won the Pulitzer Prize for his dispatches on the Battle for the Solomons. This article is largely based on a series of on-the-scene invasion dispatches he wrote for the North American Newspaper Alliance.

This Normandy beachhead of ours is the fourth beachhead I have been on in the last two years. All beachheads are unlike anything else on earth. Thousands of things are going on at once, from life to death, from hysterical triumph to crushing failure. Night is different from day only because the light is poorer, the tracer bullets more lurid, the waves creamier and your particular task either harder or easier. You work until your job is done or your superior feels too exhausted to work you any longer. Then you sleep until prodded awake by explosions or bullets or some other urgency.

Our first view of France, from the U.S. Coast Guard troop transport that carried us across the Channel, was that reflected by anti-aircraft shells lighting up the night above Normandy. It was a little past 1 a.m. on D Day, and paratroopers were beginning to land, their planes showered by whole buckets of blazing shells and golf-ball flak. One plane went down, then another and another, in plain sight of our ship, while our men stood silently in the darkness, their faces grim and their hearts sick.

The transport anchored about 11 miles offshore, and at dawn, after a terrific naval and air bombardment of the beaches, we transferred to small boats for the landing. The boats were being thrown five and ten feet into the air and digging deep into the troughs between the waves, and the leap from the slippery ladder to a greasy hatch had to be timed nicely.

To the right and left and ahead and behind, farther than a man could see, the scene was the same—a spreading mass of ships lying to, waiting patiently as cows to be unloaded, each deep laden and teeming with men and goods. The waters between them were teeming too, with small boats threading back and forth and hanging to the sides of the larger vessels like the metal spangles of a tambourine.

We passed under a sky full of airplanes laid layer upon layer on top of each other. We passed warships bombarding the enemy, and saw the splashes of enemy shells trying to hit the ships. An inferno was brewing on the beach; smoke was clotting up from it, and blinding white and orange blasts of explosions flickered hotly.

Then the war reached out a giant paw and struck dead ahead of us. There was a big explosion. Gray smoke and white water rose hundreds of feet into the air. Out of its center a mortally stricken minesweeper plunged and tilted, bleeding oil in spouts as if an artery had been severed. Then it righted itself and lay quietly, with the big gaseous-looking bubbling that ships make when they die.

Standing by to pick up survivors, we came first to those who had been blown farthest by the explosion. They were all dead. "Leave the dead and take the living first," cried Lieutenant John Tripson.

And then, from all over the sea around us, sounding small

and childlike in the wild world of waters, came cries of "Help! Help!" and one startling, pathetic cry of "Please help me!"

Big John Tripson is a Mississippi boy who used to play football for the Detroit Lions. His strength came in handy now. The wet boys in the sea with all they had on them weighed up to 300 pounds. Big John reached out and scooped them up with one hand, holding onto the boat with the other. We fished six out of the water, two of them uninjured, taking only the living and leaving the dead awash like derelicts in the unheeding sea. One man was naked. Every stitch of clothing, including his shoes and socks, had been blown off and his body was welted all over as if he had been thrashed by a cat-o'-nine-tails.

Other rescue ships had come alongside the minesweeper now, and we stood out again on our mission. Close to us was the U.S. cruiser *Tuscaloosa*. A German battery had challenged her, and she and an American destroyer had taken up the challenge. The Germans were using a very fine smokeless powder that made it impossible to spot their gun sites unless one happened to be looking right there when the muzzle flash gave them away. They also had some kind of bellows arrangement that puffed out a billow of gun smoke from a position safely removed from the actual battery. This was to throw off the spotters. But their best protection was the casements of earth-and-concrete 12½ feet thick.

The affair between the battery and the warships had the color of a duel to it. When the Germans threw down the gauntlet, you could see the gauntlet splash in the water. It was a range-finding shell. Then the shells started walking toward our warship, in a straight line. If you followed them on back you would eventually get to the battery. This was what our warship commanders were trying to do. It was a race between skills. If the Germans landed on the ship before our gunners could plot the line of their shells, then they would win. If our gunners could calculate more rapidly, then *we* would win.

Captain Waller, in command of the *Tuscaloosa*, held his $15,000,000 warship steady, setting it up as bait to keep the Germans shooting while his gunners worked out their calculations.

The destroyer—I could not identify it—stuck right with our cruiser. The splashes kept coming closer. Our ships did not move. The splashes started at 500 yards off and then went quickly to 300 yards. Now, I thought, the warships would move. But they remained silent and motionless. The next salvo was 200 yards off. The next one would do it, the next one would get them, I was thinking. The next salvo blotted out the sides of the vessels in a whip of white water, throwing a cascade across the deck of the *Tuscaloosa*.

Now in this final second the race was at its climax. The Germans knew our ships would move. They had to guess which way, they had to race to correct range and deflection for the next salvo. Our ships had to guess what the Germans would think, and do the opposite.

The destroyer had one little last trick up its sleeve. And that tipped the whole duel our way. Its black gang down below mixed rich on fuel, and a gust of black smoke poured out of the stacks. The ship had turned into the wind, so that the smoke was carried backward. The Germans could not tell whether it was the wind doing that or the destroyer's forward speed. They decided that it was forward speed and swung their guns, and straddled perfectly the position the destroyer would have occupied had it gone forward. But the destroyer had reversed engines and gone backward.

Now the game was up for the Huns. The warships swung around in their new positions and brought their guns to bear; their shells scored direct hits, and the Germans lay silently and hopelessly in their earth.

On the first beach we touched the air smelled sweet and clean with the sea. Clouds of sea gulls swooped overhead, filling the air with a whole twitter of flute notes as they complained of the invasion by American troops. There was bleak strength here, and bare wild blowy beauty, and death over every inch of it.

The Germans had sown every single inch of the soil with mines. In 24 hours our men had cleared only narrow paths, losing 17 wounded and one dead in doing so.

They walked, slept, ate, lived and worked along those paths. When they walked they put one foot carefully before the other. When they lay along the paths to sleep they put rocks alongside themselves to keep from turning over.

We had landed in the early afternoon. The wind was dying then, and the black and gray smoke stood up in spires wherever one looked and hung in the gentle wind. Smoke came from planes that had been shot down and from mines being set off by mine detectors and from American guns and German shells. Normandy seemed to be burning.

Men were coming out of the sea continually and starting to work—digging, hammering, bulldozing, trucking, planning, ordering, surveying, shooting and being shot at. Amid the artillery and machine-gun fire, and the rush and smack of shells, you could hear typewriters making their patient clatter and telephones ringing with homey businesslike sounds.

German prisoners were coming down one side of a road while American assault infantry were going up the other side. The Americans had that odd preoccupied look of men going into battle; but they were a fine, bold, brawny sight as they swung along.

"Where are you going?" I asked one of them. "I don't know," he replied. "I'm following the man ahead." The man ahead was following the man ahead, too. Finally I asked the head of the column. "I'm following the column ahead," he said.

I laughed and he laughed, but he laughed with a jubilant sound. "Well," he told me, "it's not as bad as it sounds. We've all got the same idea in this army, and if you just follow the man ahead you're bound to get to where the doing is to be done." He looked very tan and healthy as he said this, walking along with a long-legged slouch, chewing a slab of cheese from a ration tin as if it were a cud of tobacco. He was a soldier to be proud of.

Our men would go along until fired upon. Then they would investigate what was firing on them. If they had enough force on hand to solve the problem, as the military saying goes, they solved it. If not, they contained the problem and sent for what force was needed—air, artillery or ground reinforcement.

The first French people I saw were a family of typical Norman farmers—tall, blue-eyed, sturdy and very red-cheeked. American soldiers going up to the front had left the mark of their passing on the household's dining table—chewing gum, hard candy and some cigarettes. We talked about the bombardment, and I asked how they managed to live through it.

"An act of God," they said. "But the Germans, they were worse than the bombardment."

I had forgotten what the French word for "run" is, and I asked if the German soldiers billeted in their house had "promenaded away quickly" from the bombardment. They all laughed heartily.

"The Germans," one of the men said, "promenaded from the bombardment—ZIP! The way an airplane promenades through the air."

The Germans were tough veteran fighters. You never got a chance to make more than one mistake against them. Yet they were willing to surrender and seemed only to want sufficiently strong inducement. They were veterans of duty in Russia. The Russians seem to have made them very tired of the war. They fight while they think they are winning, but it is not hard to hammer them into believing they are losing. Then they give up.

When I returned to the beach more German prisoners were being brought down to await transportation to England. The bay and its immense weight of shipping was spread out before them. A German officer, when he saw that vast mass of ships, lifted his hand and let it drop in a gesture of utter despair, as if to say, "Who can win against this?"

But the thing I remember most clearly about this long day was a particular moment in the twilight. It is a picture frozen in my mind—the way a scream sometimes seems frozen in the air.

I was aboard an LCT moving both American and German

wounded from the murderous beach. The Nazi prisoners sat silently slumped side by side with the silent Americans. We were a few hundred yards offshore when there was a low-swooping air raid which came close enough for me to feel the desperate heat of one Hun plane. It hit like a bundle of fists against my face.

Very few of the men aboard stirred. Most of them were immersed in the apathy that seizes a man when he knows he has done all he can possibly do.

A large, sooty cloud of smoke sprang up from the beach as abruptly as if prodded. Our LCT trembled all over. There was debris in that cloud—big, black, torn chunks of it—and sitting on top of the cloud, poised delicately there for a moment many feet in the air, was a truck, all intact. It was silhouetted so sharply in the twilight that I could make out its wheels. Then the blasting sound of the explosion came clapping like a huge hand against our ears.

A German officer told me the war would be over in October because the Americans and Russians could not fight longer than that. I told him that all the enlisted men among the Germans I had spoken to had agreed the war would be over in October because Germany could not hold out longer.

"Your men seem very tired of fighting," I said. "Do you have trouble convincing them that Hitler will lead them to a happy end?"

"German soldiers," he said, "fight for the Fatherland and there is no separation possible in any German mind between *Der Führer* and *Das Vaterland*."

As the officer delivered his pronouncement about Hitler

and the German mind, an enlisted man sitting next to him winked at me. I smiled broadly back at him.

Suddenly I saw a German Heinkel seemingly stuck in the air above me. I saw the first of its stick of bombs drop into the water. Then I threw myself against the iron deck. The German officer clamped down on his emotions and the pain of his wounds and stood erect to show that no German was afraid. He posed himself insolently against the rail, smoking a cigarette in a careful, graceful, stiff-handed way while one knee wilted slightly in the manner approved for gentlemen posing before a mantel. I looked away in disgust from this Nazi superman across the open deck where the brown-blanketed seriously wounded lay in silent rows.

As we made our way out into the darkening sea we could see fires springing up from the town of Montebourg. The fires were the work of the *Tuscaloosa*—or, as I found out later when I got aboard the vessel, more specifically the work of the Army's Lieutenant Joe PuGash, of Tampa, serving as spotter with a naval shore fire control party; and Lieutenants Theral O'Bryant, of Tampa, and William Braybrook, of Ohio, sitting deep in the ship, in the plotting room. These boys had been talking to each other over the radio.

"German infantry is entrenching itself in the main square of the town," Joe said. "Let's ginger them up." The guns fired.

"Cease firing; mission successful, old boy," said Joe.

Two roads lead into Montebourg. The Germans were shoveling reinforcements down from Valognes. Joe was changing places to get a line on these roads when suddenly, in a very abrupt way, he gave a target and cried, "Open fire!"

Immediately afterward there was silence from him.

O'Bryant sat listening to the silence from Joe for a long time. A British voice from a plane overhead brought him back to work.

"There are transports coming into town, troops getting out of trucks and taking up positions near a cemetery there." The voice was tranquil and most British. "Would you care for a go at them?"

After the *Tuscaloosa* had fired a salvo the British voice lost most of its tranquillity. "Beautiful!" it cried. "Oh, beautiful! What a lovely shot!"

It seems that ten trucks full of Huns had been blown across acres of field by a single straddle. The British voice abruptly regained its calm. "I'm afraid I'll have to be off now," it said. "My covering plane has been shot down and a Jerry is shooting at me. Good-bye all."

"The best to you and thanks," shouted O'Bryant. But he never heard the British voice again.

Instead he heard from Joe. The boy was back overlooking Montebourg.

"I couldn't keep on spotting for you," he explained. He sounded very tired. "The Germans had us in a barrel for two hours and if I had lifted my head to see what was going on I'd have got it knocked off." Joe began running around all over the place, spotting infantry positions, troop movements, observation posts and strong points. "You sure shot the hell out of them that time," he kept saying in his tired voice.

About the time we were huffing and clanking past the *Tuscaloosa*, O'Bryant came out on deck for a breather. He helped us watch Montebourg burn. "That Joe is sure building himself up a hot time there," he said.

The wounded to whom I talked gave some idea of what the day had been like. A paratrooper captain said, "When I landed I broke my leg. I had spent two years training, and four seconds after I go to work I'm out of it. I rolled into some kind of ditch. There the krautburgers were shooting at me but they didn't hit me. I waited in the ditch and thought, Well, your total contribution to the war effort is that you spared the time of a man in the burying detail by finding your own grave. A German started coming toward me. What's the German for *Kamerad*, I wondered, and remembered that *Kamerad* is the German for *Kamerad*. Then I thought, the hell with that. I'm going to get at least one lick in in this war. So I killed the German. I waited till he got close and aimed for his groin and walked my tommygun right up the middle to his chin. Then I passed out. But I got one. My training wasn't altogether wasted."

A naval officer, suffering from exposure, said: "The whole stern blew up. You know, it's a funny thing. There was a kid blown higher than the mast. I saw him in the air, arms flailing around, legs kicking, and recognized his face there in the air. That kid was picked up later and all he had was a broken leg."

A glider pilot, shot down behind German lines, said, "I walked all night. I went toward where the guns were shooting and then I met a Frenchman. I gave him my rations and he gave me wine.

"Boy, did I get drunk! I walked through the whole German lines—and our lines, too—drunk as a goat and singing."

There is no way to record all the events that take place in a typical beachhead day, not even in a typical beachhead hour. There are hundreds of thousands of men in and around this beachhead, and if each made a record of what startling violent things he saw the records would differ in hundreds of thousands of ways.

Sergeant Erwin
and the Blazing Bomb

BY COREY FORD

Sometimes I'm asked which I like best of all the pieces I've written. I guess the answer is something I wrote one night back in 1945, on the island of Guam. It was never published; I didn't even sign it; but it was more rewarding than anything else I've ever done.

Guam was our base in the Marianas from which the B-29's took off for their nightly incendiary raids on Japan. As an Air Force colonel, I had flown with them, and I knew what those missions were like. The seven endless hours over the Pacific to the hostile coastline. The wink of ack-ack guns and the flak bursts all around us, the ground searchlights that lighted up our cabin as though an auto had parked beside us in the sky, and, after our bomb run, the red ruin of an enemy city burning. We would throttle down to cruising speed; there were 1500 miles of empty ocean between us and home.

This particular night I was not flying. I sat in the Group headquarters tent with Col. Carl Storrie, waiting for the mission's strike report. Storrie, a lean tough Texan, was the Group Commander, and he paced up and down the tent, restless as a caged animal, as the first news filtered in. The lead plane, commanded by Capt. Tony Simeral, had been forced to turn away from the target, and had made an emergency landing at Iwo Jima. It was on its way back to Guam now.

We could make out the drone of its engines, see the red flares that signaled distress, and hear the fire trucks rumbling out to meet it as it touched down. A few moments later Captain Simeral entered the tent. His face was white; he seemed to be in a state of shock. He fumbled for a cigarette with his left hand, and I saw that the back of his right hand was pockmarked with deep ugly holes that had burned clear to the bone. He took several drags before he could trust himself to talk.

It had happened as they approached the enemy coast, he said. They were flying the pathfinder plane, which drops a phosphorus smoke bomb to assemble the formation before proceeding to the target. On a B-29 this task is performed by the radio operator, back in the waist of the plane. At a signal from the pilot he releases the bomb through a narrow tube.

The radio operator on Simeral's plane was a chunky, red-haired youngster from Alabama, Staff Sgt. Henry Erwin. His crewmates liked to mimic his soft southern drawl, and he was always with a grin, always quiet and courteous. He received the routine order from Simeral, triggered the bomb and dropped it down the tube.

There was a malfunction. The bomb exploded in the tube and bounced back into Erwin's face, blinding both eyes and searing off an ear.

Phosphorus burns with a furious intensity that melts metal

like butter. Now the bomb at Erwin's feet was eating its way rapidly through the deck of the plane, toward the full load of incendiaries in their racks below. He was alone; the navigator had gone up to the astrodome to get a star shot. There was no time to think. He picked up the white-hot bomb in his bare hands, and started forward to the cockpit, groping his way with elbows and feet.

The navigator's folding table was down and latched, blocking the narrow passageway. Erwin hugged the blazing bomb under an arm, feeling it devour the flesh on his ribs, unfastened the spring latch and lifted the table. (We inspected the plane later; the skin of his entire hand was seared onto the table.)

He stumbled on, a walking torch. His clothes, hair and flesh were ablaze.

The dense smoke had filled the airplane, and Simeral had opened the window beside him to clear the air. "I couldn't see Erwin," he told us, "but I heard his voice right at my elbow. He said—" Simeral paused a moment to steady his own voice. "He said, 'Pardon me, sir' and reached across to the window and tossed out the bomb. Then he collapsed on the flight deck." A fire extinguisher was turned on him, but the phosphorus still burned.

Simeral's instrument panel was obliterated by the smoke, and the plane was out of control. It was less than 300 feet off the water when he righted it. He called to the formation that he was aborting, jettisoned his bombs and headed back to the field hospital at Iwo, three hours away. The crew applied first aid to Erwin, gave him plasma, smeared grease on his smoldering flesh. "He never lost consciousness, but he spoke only once the whole way back. He asked me—" Simeral took another drag on his cigarette. " 'Is everybody else all right, sir?' "

At Iwo, he was still exhaling phosphorus smoke from his lungs, and his body had become so rigid that he had to be eased out through the window like a log. They carried him to the hospital. When they removed the unguent pads there and exposed his flesh to the air, it began to smolder again. The airplane flew on to Guam—with 11 men who would not be living save for the one they left behind.

Simeral finished talking. A young lieutenant looked at the holes in his right hand, where the phosphorus had spattered, and said tactlessly, "You ought to put in for a Purple Heart, Captain." Simeral, his control snapping, took a wild swing at him. Then the flight surgeon arrived and gave him a sedative, and led him away to have his burns treated.

We spent the rest of the night writing up a recommendation for the Congressional Medal of Honor. It was simply worded. There was no need to speak of heroism and sacrifice; the facts were enough. It ended with the conventional military phrase: "Above and beyond the call of duty," but that seemed to express it pretty well. At five in the morning Colonel Storrie carried the single typewritten page to Air Force headquarters. Gen. Curtis LeMay was awakened. He read and signed it, and the recommendation was flashed to Washington. The reply arrived in record time: Approved.

Iwo reported that Sergeant Erwin was still alive, but no one could say how much longer he would survive. There was no Congressional Medal of Honor on Guam; the nearest was in

Honolulu, and a special B-29 was dispatched to fly the Pacific to Hawaii.

The medal was in a locked display case in Gen. Robert C. Richardson's headquarters, and the key was missing. They smashed the glass, took the medal from the case and sped back to Guam. General LeMay flew to Iwo and personally presented it to Sergeant Erwin, in a ceremony at his bedside. He repeated the final line about the call of duty, and Erwin said, "Thank you, sir."

Several years after the war I heard that Erwin was back in Alabama, happily married; he had regained the use of his hands and partial vision in one eye. I hope he can read over his citation now and then. I hope it gives him as much satisfaction as it gave me to write it.

★ ★ ★

No Medals for Joe

BY MAYO SIMON

The December sun was barely edging over the horizon when Joe Bulgo, a 21-year-old shipyard worker, walked through the gates of Honolulu's Pearl Harbor Navy Yard. It was Sunday morning, so the big shop buildings and repair basin were nearly deserted. Beyond them lay the entire Pacific Battleship Fleet, peacefully at anchor.

Joe had come to this base from a pineapple plantation on the island of Maui, where he was born. At six feet, with broad shoulders and thick arms, he seemed never to tire, and never complained. He would do any job, anytime. After all, he had taken an oath to do what the Navy said.

Today his orders were to caulk and test a new sea valve on the destroyer *Shaw*. He changed into his work clothes and picked up his pneumatic hammer, the biggest one made. When other workers tried to use this chipping gun, it would fly out of their hands. But Joe could hold it. On his way to the vessel, he heard a ship's band playing "The Star-Spangled Banner" for the morning flag-raising.

Then a familiar drone filled the sky. When Joe saw waves of aircraft flying in formation across the harbor, he assumed it was an Army exercise. He thought, *I didn't know we had that many planes.* But within seconds, plumes of water began kicking up among the ships, and he saw the planes' insignia: the rising sun.

Pandemonium broke loose, and Joe ran for cover. Screaming planes swooped low, bombing and strafing the docks and harbor. The *Shaw* rose up in a fiery cloud, its bow blown off. Torpedoes shuddered into the *Oklahoma;* the *Arizona* exploded. Ship after ship—destroyers, cruisers, minelayers—turned over and sank.

After two hours of hell, the invaders vanished, leaving behind an eerie silence—and unbelievable destruction. All the workers were enraged. They wanted to fight back, but had nothing to fight back with. Eventually Joe received new orders.

"Get down to the dock with your chipping outfit," a supervisor shouted to him. "They want you on the *Oklahoma!*"

A launch took him across the channel. Half obscured by black clouds of smoke, battleships were settling to the bottom of the harbor. Hundreds of bodies floated in the water. The *Arizona* was burning, huge flames engulfing its twisted superstructure.

The *Oklahoma* was unrecognizable. All that was left of the huge ship was a curving piece of hull sticking out of the water. It looked like a stranded gray whale.

Standing on the hull under the smoky sky were the chipping gang from Shop 11 and Joe's boss, Julio DeCastro. "Come on," he yelled at Joe. "Let's get going!"

At least three torpedoes had capsized the *Oklahoma,* DeCastro told Joe. Its masts were stuck in the mud at the bottom of the harbor, and some 400 sailors were still inside. "Listen," DeCastro said. Joe could hear the trapped sailors tapping on the steel beneath his feet.

The workers tried to cut into the hull with their chipping guns, but it was hard going. "Chipping guns not made to cut through steel this thick," Joe finally told DeCastro. "Why not burn them out?"

DeCastro showed him an open black patch in the hull. Before he arrived, the burner gang from a Navy ship had tried using acetylene torches. A cork-lined compartment had been set afire, and two trapped sailors had suffocated. "We have no choice," said DeCastro.

Joe started up his gun with an earsplitting clatter. He leaned into the bulkhead, made two cuts and helped bend out a patch. Then he went down into the ship and relieved several exhausted workers chipping at a deck inside.

It was boiling hot. No air. They kept looking for a way to get to the trapped men. But the ship was upside down, and it was impossible to figure where they were. As they drilled, they hit oil tanks, waste tanks, dead ends, and would have to plug up and start over. They knew that, little by little, they were letting out all the ship's trapped air—the only thing keeping the water level down. The more holes they made, the closer the men were to drowning.

Joe worked tirelessly, opening bulkhead after bulkhead, only to find himself in a maze of tiny compartments filled with debris. Sometimes he came upon smashed bodies of sailors in passageways, but he had to keep going.

Whenever Joe paused, he could hear desperate tapping reverberating through the ship. *Save me, save me,* the terrified sailors were saying. *Give me life. . . .* That sound would live in Joe's marrow forever.

Night fell, and the clatter of the chipping guns continued. Fully expecting another Japanese attack, the workers could not use lights on the hull. Instead, they relied on the grisly illumination from the burning *Arizona.*

Toward midnight, when Joe cut into the hull, water bubbled out. He tasted it: sweet. He had hit a freshwater tank. DeCastro found a pump, and after several agonizing hours, they had removed enough water so they could crawl into the tank.

They drilled open its bottom, and a shout went up: inside was a dry, white shaft. *A way in!*

As the others unreeled the hose of his pneumatic hammer, Joe cautiously slid into the shaft with only a cage lantern to light his way. Deeper and deeper he went past the ribs of the upside-down ship. He felt like Jonah in the belly of the whale.

Suddenly the ship began to sway and groan. Joe's stomach tightened in terror. *If it starts to settle, I'm gone.* Fighting the urge to turn back, he tried to catch his breath in the choking stench of oil and sewage.

Then he heard the tapping. Faint. Steady. Joe tapped back with his chisel on the sweating metal bulkhead. *Come on,* he thought. *Tell me where you are.* Finally, answering taps. Joe slid down farther and cocked his head, listening hard. He called for help from DeCastro. The two lifted open a manhole cover, and Joe slipped into an empty compartment. He heard the sound once more. *Tap tap tap.* It was coming from the other side of the bulkhead.

Joe tapped again. Suddenly voices were shouting: "Hurry! Water's coming up!"

Joe's chipping gun dug into the steel with an angry clatter. When trapped air came out with a *whoosh*, the sailors tried to stop it with their fingers. "Don't do that!" Joe yelled. "I'm going to cut it fast." He was a good worker, but he'd never cut so rapidly in his life.

Water was rising to Joe's waist now. But he refused to be distracted from his work. *Keep on going,* he told himself. *Get them out.*

After cutting three sides, Joe was able to pry open the steel. Immediately the sailors came out in a huge rush of water—kids smeared with oil, hardly able to move or breathe after being trapped for over 20 hours. None had the strength to get to the hatch. So Joe said, "Here, up on my back!"

One by one they climbed on his broad back, and he lifted them to the hatch, where other workers pulled them to safety. By the time the last sailor got out, the water was up to Joe's neck. He scrambled up his hose line, and DeCastro sealed the hatch behind him.

Joe blinked in the sunlight, filling his lungs with fresh air. The sailors, wrapped in blankets, were already in the launch that was taking them to the hospital ship. Joe shouted and waved, but they were too far away to hear. He watched them disappear across the gray harbor.

All told, more than 400 died in the sunken ship; but over four days and nights, Joe Bulgo and the rest of the chipping gang saved 32 men. Later that year, Navy citations "for heroic work with utter disregard of personal safety" were awarded to Joe Bulgo, Julio DeCastro and 18 others from Shop 11.

After the war, Joe married, had four children and joined the merchant marine. During the Vietnam war, he returned to work for the Navy on a chipping gang at the San Francisco Bay Naval Shipyard. When his family said he was working too hard, he'd reply, "Our boys are over there dying. They need these ships."

In 1971, he had his first heart attack. After a second attack, he retired.

The most precious thing he owned, his citation, was lost when somebody stole his suitcase in a bus station. He wrote letter after letter to Washington. He finally got a copy of the citation, with a letter saying he might have a medal coming. He waited, wrote more letters. Nothing happened. It seemed the rescue was a forgotten episode about a forgotten ship.

That was the story Joe Bulgo told me in 1986 when I turned up at his door, 45 years after Pearl Harbor. I kept thinking to myself: *This man deserves a medal. Well, if nothing else, the film will give him and his fellow shipyard workers the recognition they merit.*

But the film was never made, the idea shelved by the network. Discouraged, I put everything away—the script, my notes, the documents, the reminiscences of sailors—and I went on to something else.

Almost a year later, I got a call from Al Ellis of the U.S.S.

Oklahoma Association, an organization for everyone who had ever served on the ship. Would I speak at their next convention in San Jose?

I was about to politely decline when I remembered something Joe had told me. At the end of the interview, he had said, "You know, I never seen any of those boys I saved. It was all in the dark and so quick. I wish I could have talked with them once."

On May 16, 1987, I waited in the San Jose hotel, where 200 ex-sailors and their wives were meeting. I knew Joe was coming—his wife, Val, had told me how excited he was to have been invited—but I also knew he was ill. Bone cancer, she had said.

Even so, when Val and their daughter, Linda, brought Joe into the big convention room, I was shocked. He was in a wheelchair. His once-powerful body had shrunk. His eyes were filled with pain. "How you doing, Joe?" I said. He pulled my head down and whispered, "Thinking about this night is what's kept me alive."

They seated the Bulgo family in front of the head table. A Navy chaplain gave the invocation. We ate. The master of ceremonies told jokes. Then a band started to play, and everyone was laughing, drinking, dancing. Joe sat stiffly in his chair, his food untouched. I wondered, *Will people actually want to listen to an old war story?*

Finally they introduced me, and I began to speak. I told them one sailor's story from that dark December day at Pearl Harbor. How he and ten others had been trapped in a compartment slowly filling with water. How for 27 hours they'd banged frantically against the bulkhead, hoping—praying—that someone might save them. And how, finally, a young worker had cut through the bulkhead, releasing them all. I described how the rescuer, in the accent of the islands, had said to the sailors, "Here, on my back"—and then lifted each one to safety.

The crowd was quiet as I read off the names of the sailors rescued that day. "I know three of those men are here tonight. And I also know you never got a chance to thank him. So if there's something you'd like to say to the Hawaiian kid who risked his life to save yours 46 years ago—well, he's right over there."

It is impossible to describe the emotions that swept the hall as I pointed to Joe, and 200 people rose to their feet, cheering. He covered his face with his napkin. He didn't want them to see him crying. Then three elderly veterans embraced the man who could no longer stand, even to acknowledge the applause, but on whose broad, strong back they had once been carried.

Joe Bulgo died two months later. When the San Francisco *Examiner* called me, I told them what I knew. His obituary begins: "Joseph Bulgo, Jr., a neglected hero of Pearl Harbor . . ."

Well, yes—there hadn't been any medals for Joe. But, I thought to myself, in the end we made things right. We said thank you, at last, to an American hero.

★ ★ ★

Hero of Sugar Loaf Hill

BY MALCOLM McCONNELL

In Kentfield, California, Mark Stebbins was sorting through his deceased uncle's papers when he came upon a box marked "Jim Day." He recognized the name of a Marine who had served with his uncle. Stebbins glanced quickly through the box. It was full of old, smeared copies of what seemed to be a report.

The papers were a recommendation for the Medal of Honor, including vivid witness accounts of savage combat in the Pacific. But the report had never been acted upon—and a brave Marine had never received the honor due him. Was it too late?

By dawn of May 14, 1945, the Marines of Second Battalion, 22nd Regiment, had been pinned down on Okinawa for some 30 hours. The Japanese commanded a series of hills along a narrow section of the island, raining machine-gun and artillery fire down on the Americans.

Cpl. Jim Day, 19, was ordered to try to hold the western slope of Sugar Loaf Hill, a steep hummock of gravelly mud that looked like a huge overturned bathtub. If the height could be secured, the enemy's cross fire would be disrupted, allowing the Americans to punch through.

When the young man from Overland, Missouri, quit high school to join the Marines two years earlier, he was 17, five-foot-six and 130 pounds. Now, five months from his 20th birthday, he had grown to a full six feet—and was a survivor of bloody fighting on Eniwetak and Guam.

Day and his men crunched up the hillside through heavy artillery fire. Finally they stumbled into a 30-foot crater almost five feet deep, dug by a bomb or a shell. They felt lucky to find cover, but almost instantly more than 20 Japanese soldiers attacked. As Day's squad rose to defend their position, they were hit by bullets and shrapnel. Day felt searing metal tear across his arms.

Rolling and bobbing, he jammed fresh clips into his rifle, then threw grenades, aiming short so they'd bounce down among the enemy before exploding. After a furious firefight, the attack was beaten back.

His ears still ringing, Day heard moaning behind him. Of the eight men who'd made it with him to the crater, three were dead, three wounded. Another, Pfc. Dale Bertoli, was writhing in pain. "You hit, Bert?" Day asked.

"It's the fever," Bertoli gasped. He had returned to the front lines only that morning after a debilitating bout of dengue fever. It had surged back, rendering the husky Marine almost powerless with spasms and a crippling headache.

Minutes later Sgt. Narolian West and two stretcher-bearers slid into the crater. Immediately the Japanese launched a second assault. Day spun around and shot three enemy soldiers who had dashed unseen to the hole. Their bodies tumbled onto West.

During the melee two of the wounded Marines died. "Come

on back with us," West now begged. Day refused. So did Bertoli and a badly wounded replacement named McDonald.

Night fell. Japanese soldiers slid under the chalky light of flares. Day waited until he could hear them coming up the hill. Then he threw grenades at the shadows.

With daylight the slope around the crater was pounded with mortar fire. When the barrage lifted, enemy soldiers surged up the slope. Day rose to fire and cut down the attackers.

This lonely outpost ahead of the main American lines put Day and his two comrades in a critical position. To reinforce their hill strongholds, enemy troops would have to cross open lowlands exposed to Day's fire. By holding off the Japanese, he gave the Americans time to find a way to push through. The Japanese knew it and were determined to drive them off Sugar Loaf Hill.

Late in the afternoon of May 15 another attack began. Day and McDonald were perched on the edge of the crater, firing long bursts down the slope, when a Japanese anti-tank gun cracked. McDonald was killed instantly. Shrapnel riddled Day's hands. Ignoring the pain, Day dragged a machine gun to the right lip of the crater and fired until the attackers retreated.

That night they faced a new peril: American phosphorus mortar shells exploded around the hole like a Fourth of July fireworks display gone bad. Day smothered flaming chunks on Bertoli's neck and arms with handfuls of mud. He felt stabbing heat in his right foot as a chunk of molten phosphorus burned through his shoe. Ripping it off, Day covered his foot with mud. The two men sprawled in the crater, floating on pain and exhaustion.

At dawn, May 16, a cloying white mist rose from the valleys. Day heard the faint scrape of boots. By the time he could hoist his rifle, the enemy soldiers were only 40 feet away. He cut several down and drove the rest off.

The day drifted by in bursts of noise and sudden, ringing silence. Flies swarmed in a hot stench of death. At nightfall Day fought to stay awake, firing at the enemy and taking out two machine-gun crews. Then it was morning, and a Marine lieutenant suddenly dropped into the crater, his feet crunching on hundreds of empty brass shell casings and tinkling steel grenade spoons. "Pull back, Corporal," he ordered, shouting so the deafened Day could understand. An American battalion was now sweeping their way.

Day and Bertoli staggered down the slope through the advancing column. The Marines who finally relieved them counted dozens of enemy dead.

Day's defense of Sugar Loaf Hill for three days and nights would prove to be key to smashing the enemy's line across Okinawa. His battalion commander, Lt. Col. Horatio Woodhouse, immediately ordered witness statements to be taken from survivors in order to recommend the young man for the Medal of Honor. "Time is critical and events fleeting in our current situation," Woodhouse noted. Witnesses who were alive one day could be killed the next.

Seven statements were collected, and a citation was drafted. Then the war brutally intervened. Woodhouse and Bertoli were killed in battle, and Day was badly wounded. His Medal of Honor recommendation never moved up the chain of command.

After the war Day re-enlisted. Whenever new Marines would ask him about combat in the Pacific, Day would offer few details.

In the Korean War, Lieutenant Day led a platoon in hand-to-hand fighting, earning two Silver Star Medals and two Purple Hearts. In Vietnam, Maj. Jim Day earned another Silver Star and his sixth Purple Heart. In 1974 Colonel Day took command of the Fourth Marine Corps District in Philadelphia.

That year Owen Stebbins, who had been Day's company commander on Okinawa, heard about the lost Medal of Honor recommendation. Stebbins had been wounded and evacuated from the battlefield just before Day's heroic action. He had never seen the citation. Now he called Day and told him he wanted to resubmit the report.

Day demurred. "Okinawa was a long time ago," he said.

Stebbins nevertheless worked doggedly over the years to secure medals for the forgotten Marines of Sugar Loaf Hill, including a posthumous Bronze Star Medal for Dale Bertoli and several other enlisted men. Finally, in September 1995, Stebbins wrote Day, who had retired from the Marines at the rank of major general and was running a home construction business in California. "I'm going ahead," Stebbins said. "You'll never do anything about it yourself."

Stebbins forwarded the recommendation to Marine Corps headquarters in Washington, D.C. But like many of his comrades, Stebbins did not get to see Day receive his award. He died in 1996.

Soon afterward his nephew, Mark Stebbins, found the box of Day's records among his uncle's effects. He did not realize the import of the papers, but he tracked down Day and sent him the box.

Meanwhile Marine Corps officials debated whether to proceed with Day's medal. Most of the men who had signed the statements were dead, so there needed to be evidence of the documents' authenticity.

Finally, an Awards Branch investigator found the service records of each witness in the military archives of the National Personnel Records Center in St. Louis. And there, in each yellowing folder, lay a carbon copy identical to those in Day's report, corroborating every word.

On January 20, 1998, Maj. Gen. James Day (Ret.) stood in the East Room of the White House. Among the Marines who had gathered to see him receive the Medal of Honor were his son Lt. Col. James A. Day, and his grandson Lance Cpl. Joshua Eustice.

"General," President Clinton said, "you are the embodiment of the motto 'Semper Fidelis.' You have been unerringly faithful to those who fought alongside you, to the Corps and to the United States.

"We are profoundly fortunate to count you among our heroes."

★ ★ ★

On a Wing and a Prayer

BY LAURA ELLIOTT
Condensed from *Washingtonian* Magazine

The morning of December 15, 1944, Martha Blanton Elliott sat at her kitchen table preparing a fruitcake for the holidays, just as she had done for dozens of years. Keeping to rituals comforted mothers whose boys were fighting and dying overseas.

But for Martha, comfort came hard. Her only son, Jack, a co-pilot on a B-24 bomber, had been shot down over Germany nine months earlier and was reported missing in action. There were no details in the telegram from the War Department—no mention if parachutes had been seen after Jack's plane was crippled, nothing that could stop the terrible scenarios flickering through her head. She wondered how it was that she hadn't felt him fall from the skies, how she could have been playing bridge on the day her son must have been so afraid.

Martha prayed that a compassionate German mother had found her boy and helped him. Then she tried not to think about it. She helped her husband, "Big Jack," collect eggs, feed the chickens and prepare to seed the fields on their 168-acre farm outside Richmond, Virginia. She continued volunteering for the Red Cross. Martha knew that was what her son would want her to do.

Second Lt. Jack Elliott was at 25,000 feet over northern France heading for armaments plants in Friedrichshafen, Germany, when his B-24 was hit. The left wing was ablaze as he moved as quickly as he could in his fleece-lined flight suit to the open bomb-bay doors, shimmied down among the 500-pound bombs and dropped into the clouds.

His parachute opened and jerked his free fall into a float. Blown clear of the clouds, Jack looked down and saw a smooth landscape of snow. *Snow? Maybe I'm in Switzerland.*

Pain ripped his left leg on impact. He limped to a bramble, stuffed his chute into its roots and covered it with snow. Pulling an escape kit from his pants pocket, he ate part of the C rations and, wincing, shot a syringe of morphine into his shin. Then, using a small compass, he began walking west, away from Germany.

After a while, he saw an elderly figure approaching on a bicycle. Knowing he couldn't move fast enough on his ankle to hide, he decided to ask for help. The old man dragged his foot on the gravel to stop but said nothing. Relying on his college French, Jack blurted, *"J'aime America."*

"Yank," the man replied.

Jack had fallen onto the edge of France, where it meets Germany and Switzerland. The Frenchman was a teacher, which explained his command of English. By pure luck, he was also an Allied sympathizer.

He hid Jack in the loft of a village school and brought him bread, cheese and clothing. Jack's ankle had ballooned to three times its normal size and was streaked purple and red. They had to cut off his boot.

"It looks broken," muttered the old man. "We'll have to get you to Bern to a hospital. You sleep."

Jack hunkered down in the hay and tried not to think about his parents, tried not to see his mother's face when she received the War Department telegram. His leg shaking with pain, he gave himself a second shot of morphine.

The Frenchman woke him before daybreak. With Jack perched on the bicycle's handlebars, they rode until they neared the Swiss border. "Go through the woods while I bribe the guards," the Frenchman directed. "Walk quickly and crawl under the barbed wire. Keep straight until you come to a road. I will wait there."

Jack limped along, his ankle throbbing. Then he started second-guessing himself. What if he had gone the wrong way? What if they had arrested the teacher?

It was his first lesson in underground trust. Ask no questions, do as you're told, keep moving no matter what. Finally, he came to a clearing. There sat the old man. "You took a long time" was all he said.

Two more days brought them to Bern. When they reached the hospital gate, the Frenchman vanished. That was Jack's second lesson in how the underground operated. The French didn't want thanks, didn't want to know names or remember faces. That way, if they were caught, information couldn't be beaten out of them.

When Jack could travel, he and two other Americans were spirited across the mountains to Lausanne. They would then cross Lake Geneva to France and try to make it back to their units via Spain or Portugal.

The first thing the French did was to split up the airmen. Jack was moved to Annecy and given instructions in hesitant English. "Never take a main road. Don't whistle—French don't whistle. Never walk into a town. Someone will meet you before. If not, go around. Never double back. If you come to a fork before you are picked up, take the right-hand path. Don't rely on signs. We move them to confuse the Germans."

Next, they replaced his American shoes with hard, wooden-sole ones and blackened his sandy-colored hair with soot. He had to look like a peasant.

His instructions were to follow a trail to a certain town. "You will be picked up after passing a farmhouse with red window boxes and a cow tied to the gate," he was told.

"How will I know my contact?" Jack asked.

The Frenchman smiled as he left. "You won't."

What the French had not prepared Jack for was how self-conscious he would feel, how vulnerable. In the dark, the crunch of each step carried like the sound of a saw going through hard oak. He suppressed the urge to whistle to calm himself.

Every sound he heard made his skin crawl—the breeze rattling leaves, the shift of a twig as an animal skittered away. Finally, at dawn, he thought he saw the farmhouse. But no one came out. *What do I do now?*

Suddenly, a child appeared—out of nowhere. *Don't look scared. Keep moving. He's just a kid.*

The boy was walking toward him despite the wide berth Jack was giving him. As Jack tried to pass with a tip of his cap, the child took his hand. Jack looked at him, ashamed that his own hand was trembling. The boy, who couldn't have been more than seven, led him, without a word, to a house and hid him in the attic.

From then on, Jack walked and lived by night, and hid by day in haylofts and cellars. The sound of his own voice became alien to him. He was dirty, hungry and alone. As he passed under the windows of houses, his greatest fear was that his rumbling stomach would betray him.

One evening, he spotted a German patrol. He had no choice but to head straight into the village he was trying to skirt. When he turned a corner and saw still more soldiers, he slipped into a cafe. Nauseated by the smell of food and cigarettes, he staggered to the bar. *"Bière,"* he muttered to the bartender.

Jack could feel the stare of the man next to him. Trying not to return it, he reached into his pocket for a Swiss franc, the only money he had. The man closed his hand over Jack's and laid a French coin on the counter.

When the man left, Jack followed. "Keep going wherever they told you," he whispered and disappeared down a cobblestone alley.

German patrols were everywhere now. One day, Jack was forced to take a trolley. He was holding an overhead strap when he noticed a man staring at his arm and shaking his head. Jack looked up and saw the bracelet, etched with pilot wings, his mother had given him. He switched hands. The man smiled and went back to reading.

When he finally reached the Pyrenees, Jack was reunited

with the two airmen to cross the border with a Spanish guide. Halfway over the pass, the traitorous guide led them to a waiting German patrol and collected his reward.

The Germans put their three prisoners onto a train heading north. After riding for hours, they heard a loud explosion. Air raid! Their guard was looking out, aiming his gun upward, when the Americans overpowered him and escaped. Jack never saw his companions again.

Once more, he had no idea where he was or what to do. Suddenly, a German soldier appeared. Then two more, guns drawn. Jack was driven to a house on the outskirts of a town and locked in an unlit cellar.

He lost track of time in the Gestapo interrogations he endured. He was grateful that everything had been kept shrouded; he couldn't betray his saviors, even under torture. Maybe a week went by. Maybe ten days. He wondered how long it would take him to die. Then one night—or was it day?—he and his cellmate decided to attempt escape. They communicated their plan to each other with gestures.

Jack feigned sickness. His cellmate killed the guard who came to investigate Jack's cries, then put on the Nazi's uniform and dragged Jack out to "shoot" him. The guards jeered as Jack pretended to sob and plead for his life. Once in the fields, the two split up and ran.

Hurrying down the road, Jack saw an elderly lady struggling with an umbrella and two Germans coming on motorcycles. Jack walked up to her, opened the umbrella, and held it over her head as the Germans rode past.

The lady smiled at him. She had the sweetest face and smelled of lilac, like his mother. She nodded toward a steeple, clasped her hands in prayer and said, *"L'église."* She squeezed his hand as she took the umbrella and tottered away.

Jack followed the sound of an organ to a small Catholic chapel, where people were gathered for Mass. *Please help me,* was all he could think to pray as he knelt in a side pew and bent his head.

Behind him, he heard the rustle of stiff material. A uniform? No, a nun—a beautiful nun. He carefully mimicked her genuflections.

"Come," she whispered at the end of the service. Behind the church were a hay cart, a mule and two men. They grinned and poured wine on Jack as the "nun" yanked off her habit. The church's bells began to ring joyfully, and she pulled Jack into the hay.

"Bonne chance," the men called, running alongside the cart as it carried the supposed newlyweds out of town. Jack was convinced he was still in his cell, dreaming.

He came to know the woman as Renee. The Germans had murdered her parents and sister, and she now ran the most ruthless underground group Jack had encountered.

In late November, Jack was crouched by a creek, trying to grab a fish. Then he felt the earth begin to tremble. He watched a dozen tanks roll by before he realized they were American. *American! My God!* He ran toward them. *Idiot,* he suddenly thought, stopping short. *Want to be shot now after all this?* Shriveled to 90 pounds, covered in grime, dressed in a French beret, torn civilian pants and jacket, he hardly looked like an American pilot.

Jack raised his hands and forced himself to walk. "Hey," he called to the soldiers following the tanks, "am I glad to see you."

Early on December 15, 1944, Jack Elliott arrived at Washington's National Airport. He caught a cab to his sister Lee's home in Fairfax, Virginia. She nearly fainted when she answered the door.

"Let me call Mom," she said. "No," Jack said. "It'll be too much of a shock."

Lee and her five-year-old daughter boarded a bus for Richmond with Jack. The girl darted along the aisle telling passengers, "Uncle Jack's home. We're going to tell Granny and keep her from having a heart attack."

They got off the bus and hailed a taxi. To Jack the eight-mile ride to the farm took an eternity.

Inside the house, Martha heard the sound of car wheels on gravel and wondered who would visit so close to dinnertime. Then she froze: the Army delivered death notices in person. She walked to the door. *Don't cry in front of a stranger*, she told herself, and looked out.

Jack's aged pointer, Speed, was dancing around a terribly thin man bent over trying to pet him. *Strange*, thought Martha, *I haven't seen Speed act that way since Jack left. Oh, my Lord.*

"Jack!" she cried out, throwing open the door.

Jack stood and opened his arms. They held each other for a long time, not saying a word. Finally, Martha pulled away and put her hand over her heart. It hurt in the most wonderful way.

She was sure it was the first time she had felt it beat since Jack left home.

Jack Elliott is my father. I've always admired his tenacity, his gutsiness during a crisis, his kindness to hurt or sick people, and his unflinching belief in the potential for good in mankind. In writing his story, I understand better what shaped those qualities.

Daddy stayed on active duty for three more years after 1944 and was in the reserves until 1969, leaving the service as a lieutenant colonel. In civilian life, he became a missile engineer. He is now retired.

He doesn't talk about the war much, but I can tell that little else in his life has had such an impact. His voice still grows husky, 49 years later, telling about the people who helped him and about one of his first duties stateside.

For a time after his return, Daddy served as an escort for funerals at Arlington National Cemetery. One was for a soldier who had died while being flown back to Walter Reed hospital for treatment. Standing by the grave were the dead soldier's mother, wife and two small children. As the honor guard fired its salute, the littlest one looked heavenward and said, "There goes my daddy."

Every few years, my father picks his way through all those tombstones to pay his respects to that mother's lost son, that child's daddy.

Those Navy Boys Changed My Life

BY CARL T. ROWAN

My history professor, Merl Eppse, stepped into the classroom and said crisply: "Rowan, come with me to the dean's office."

I was flustered by the request. I hadn't done anything bad enough, I thought, to be hauled before the dean. Warily, I followed the professor. This was in 1943, near the end of my second quarter at the all-Negro Tennessee State College in Nashville, Tennessee.

"Rowan," the dean said, "we have a chance to help crack the ban on Negro officers in the Navy. Some of Tennessee State's young men are being allowed to compete in national examinations for the Navy's officer-training program. I want you to take these exams and volunteer."

"What?" I asked in disbelief.

The Navy, one of the most strictly segregated institutions in the nation, had for the past 20 years used Negroes primarily as mess attendants and stewards. Aware of this, I hesitated, but when the dean repeated his request I reluctantly agreed. I took the exams and passed them; then after interviews by a panel of officers I was accepted for training.

Nowadays, as I watch the bitterness and strife in many communities, I think of those tense years I spent as a sailor and later as an officer. Men like me were trying to convince the Navy and the nation that it was possible—with firmness and common sense—to wipe out segregation and other social injustices without rancor and bloodshed.

My first Navy assignment was to the officer-training unit at Washburn University in Topeka, Kansas. I was the lone Negro in a unit of about 335 sailors. Almost all these young men had grown up in states where tradition decreed that the Negro was anything but their intellectual and social equal. Yet, my first night at Washburn, a chief petty officer and a lieutenant gave me a warm welcome. When young Charlie Van Horn, of Coffeyville, Kansas, learned that I was to be his roommate, he quipped: "I'll be too damned busy trying to pass this physics course to notice the pigment of your skin." And that is how it was.

I was learning for the first time that the things young men share in common far outweigh racial differences. We all hated drill, calisthenics and Saturday inspections; we all loved the weekend liberties and the endless bull sessions. Still, there were difficulties. One day as I walked into the guest room of the house in which I lived, a trainee from Ohio was sounding off about his low regard for "niggers." There was sharp silence. I just stared at the young man for a few seconds. Then I turned to a piano-playing boy from Texas named Noah Brannen and said, "Noah, I've got a new tune called 'Star Eyes.' Let's give it a try." Noah walked eagerly to the piano and a few moments later a dozen of us were bunched together trying to sing harmony.

I still remember Brannen, the Texan, sharing with me his love for music but at the same time revealing all the conflicts created within him by his background. "Where is that over-powering odor they tell me all Negroes have?" he asked one day. He seemed happy to be told that a shower has the same cleansing effect on a Negro as on a member of any other race.

The Washburn University campus was an oasis of democ-racy set in a community of many social contradictions. I could ride unsegregated on city buses, but I was barred from entering most theaters, restaurants and bowling alleys with my fellow-trainees. On several occasions my buddies took me into drug-stores and other places, saying simply by their actions that I was one of the gang. In this way, they made me the first Negro ever served in these places.

I wondered how the other "guinea pigs" in other units were making out, and later when I got to Midshipman School at Fort Schuyler in New York City, I met two of them—Theodore Chambers and Clarence McIntosh. We were pleased that there was no attempt to put us together. Everything was strictly al-phabetical, with the result that the midshipman in the bunk next to mine was a white fellow from Pascagoula, Mississippi.

He and I commiserated with each other throughout the days of close-order drills, the running from class to class, the fran-tic cramming for tests in navigation, gunnery and so on. Fort Schuyler was tough—midshipmen at other schools called it the Laundry, because so many candidates washed out.

Soon it was obvious that my Mississippi bunk mate was on the verge of washing out. One night as our company studied gunnery problems, he offered me half of his candy bar.

"Rowan, you know that I'm flunking out of this heah damned rat race," he said. "But there's one thing I gotta git off my chest first—just sort of one Southern boy to another."

Other midshipmen rolled their eyes uneasily in our direction.

"Just wanta tell you," he continued, "that a little while back, if somebody had told me I'd be sitting beside a Nigra and not minding it—I mean, appreciating it—I'da knocked his teeth out. But here I am, and I just wanta tell you and wish you luck."

I avoided washing out, as did the other two Negroes, and at the age of 19 became an ensign in the United States Naval Reserve—on what ranks as one of the triumphant days of my life. The three of us from Fort Schuyler, along with Ensign Samuel Gravely from the Midshipman School at Columbia University, were the first Negro officers with the training that qualified us for duty on ocean-going vessels.

The next test would be integration aboard ship, and here the Navy moved very cautiously. They picked auxiliary craft—fleet tankers, troop transports and so forth—for the first mixing of Negro officers and seamen (who now sported the insignia of signalmen, electricians, boatswain's mates) with whites.

I was assigned to a fast tanker, the U.S.S. *Chemung*, and given command of the communications division, a group of about 35 men of whom only two were Negroes. Several of my other men, including the chief petty officer, were Southerners.

What the Navy obviously wanted to know was whether white Southerners would take orders from a Negro officer. They did, and they executed them without the slightest hesitation.

Much of the credit must go to the captain, an Annapolis graduate. One icy, windy night in the North Atlantic as I stood the midnight to 4 a.m. watch, he came to the bridge and uttered the only sentences about race that I heard from him.

"I'm a Navy man," he said, "and we're in a war. To me, it's that stripe that counts—and the training and leadership that it is supposed to symbolize. That's why I never called a meeting of the crew to 'prepare' them, to explain their obligation to respect you, or anything like that. I didn't want anyone to think you were different from any other officer coming aboard."

The skipper had shown an acute understanding of what I—and other Negroes—wanted: no special favors, no special restrictions, just the right to rise or fall on merit.

Still there were many crew members who figured that since I was a Negro I must have been sent aboard the *Chemung* primarily to look out for the Negro crewmen. It took an unusual incident to destroy this idea.

Christmas of 1945 the *Chemung* pulled into Baltimore for holiday port. Most of the seamen dashed ashore to celebrate and only a skeleton force was kept aboard. A petty officer in my division, while on communications duty, took advantage of the situation to sneak a blonde aboard—a gross violation of regulations. It was his luck to have the captain return aboard unexpectedly.

The petty officer was summoned to Captain's Mast and crew members speculated that he would get a summary court-martial. There was scant ground for a defense, but it's an officer's duty to look out for his men. So I went before the captain with my petty officer—who was white—and helped in a stirring, though shallow, defense. The culprit escaped with a mere warning. Later I proudly accepted congratulations from the men in my division, who now realized that I was for all of them.

There are no medals of honor listed in my records at the Bureau of Personnel. But a tribute I will always remember came that summer day in 1946 when I left the *Chemung* and the Navy. At the gangplank to say good-by was a big boatswain's mate whom I'd had thrown in the brig the night he started a riot in the Virgin Islands; a signalman whom I'd quieted down with the threat of my .45 when he came aboard drunk and tried using the fire ax to extort cinnamon rolls from the baker; and a collection of other crew members, many talking in Southern drawls.

"Mr. Rowan, if you're ever in my neck of the woods, the latch string shore will be out," said a white lad from my home state, Tennessee.

"That goes double for me, and y'all know I mean it," said a radio operator from Georgia.

I walked down that gangplank in a strange daze, almost overwhelmed by mixed emotions. I was sure of one thing: the previous three years had been filled with a wonderful revolution in the life of a country boy from the wrong side of Tennessee's tracks. And I had reason to believe that the revolution was even greater in the lives of crew members from the other side of the tracks.

Today I am pleased whenever I get a letter with a postmark from Arkansas or Texas—just a note from someone who sailed the *Chemung*, writing to tell me that, for him at least, the thought of a desegregated South strikes no special terror.

During World War II, Carl T. Rowan became one of the first African Americans to become an officer in the U.S. Navy. His Navy experience revolutionized the life of a country boy from the wrong side of Tennessee's tracks—and the many shipmates he touched along the way. From there, he went on to serve in both the Kennedy and Johnson administrations as ambassador to Finland and later as director of the U.S. Information Agency.

THE KOREAN WAR

★ ★ ★

1000 Men and a Baby

BY LAWRENCE ELLIOTT

One lonely Saturday night in July 1953, a medical orderly at an Army dispensary in war-devastated Korea went out to have a smoke and kicked a bundle of newspapers out of his way. A feeble little cry shivered up from the darkness.

It was a child—a gasping, emaciated infant.

Soon the orderly was racing toward the Star of the Sea Children's Home in Inchon. There he handed the bundle to a nun who unwrapped the scrawny little body. The baby was a boy, perhaps a month old. And his eyes were blue.

The war was entering its fourth year. Inchon had been overrun, liberated, shelled and starved, and the Star of the Sea orphanage had been spared little. Staffed by overworked French nuns and a dozen Korean aides, it was run by Sister Philomena, a crafty, tough-minded Irish nurse.

Her orphanage was so desperately overburdened that when the children became teenagers they had to be sent out on their own. There was never enough food or clothing. *What would she do with this half-Caucasian baby?* She wondered.

Sister knew in her heart that there could never be a place here for a blue-eyed child. He would always be scorned as "the white one." When her back was turned, the Korean aides ignored the baby. Even if he somehow managed to grow to adulthood, she realized, he would be a pariah—despised and harassed as the abandoned offspring of an American soldier.

So when the USS *Point Cruz*—an escort carrier that had been in the thick of the action—dropped anchor in Inchon harbor early in September, Sister Philomena had an idea. She sent a message to the chaplain, Lt. Edward O. Riley.

They were old friends. Sometimes, with the connivance of the *Point Cruz's* captain, Father Riley brought the children things from the ship's stores: powdered milk, cough medicine, aspirin. When he arrived at the orphanage, Sister Philomena told him about the baby the orderly had brought her from ASCOM—the U.S. Army Service Command headquarters. Then she took him to the nursery.

Blue eyes stared up at them. The infant was all ribs and swollen abdomen. A rash covered his face. "I haven't proper medicine or food," Sister Philomena said. "Surely you can do something, Father. After all, he's an American."

Father Riley brooded about it, then went to talk to his skipper. "Does this baby have a name?" the skipper asked.

"George—after the orderly who brought him in," said the chaplain.

"What are the chances he might be adopted by a Korean family?"

"Zero."

"Then here's what I want you to do," said Capt. John T. Hayward, nicknamed Chick, who had once been expelled from a military academy, never finished high school, and thus knew something about starting out against the odds. "Find some Korean official who will issue this kid a passport. But first we're going to bring him aboard the *Point Cruz* and keep him here until he's healthy."

Father Riley was elated. But he felt obliged to ask how the Navy would take to the idea of housing an infant aboard an aircraft carrier.

"Hayward's Law," came the crisp reply, "holds that, in an emergency, regulations are to be intelligently disregarded."

"God bless you," said the chaplain gruffly, and went off to battle the Korean bureaucracy.

A week later he was back, sagging with discouragement. He had trudged all over Inchon and beseeched countless government functionaries. But no birth certificate—no passport.

Chick Hayward didn't flinch. "I guess we have to go right to the top." Taking a bottle of whiskey out of his safe, he said, "Father, this is my last bottle. Maybe you'll find someone in the foreign ministry in Seoul who needs it more than we do. Don't come back without the passport."

The hospital ship USS *Consolation* had been in port three weeks before Lt. Hugh Keenan, a surgeon from Spokane,

Washington, set foot on land. It was a blazing-hot September morning, and his two companions, old hands in Inchon, suggested visiting the Star of the Sea orphanage. "We can get out of the sun and Sister Philomena will give us tea."

But Sister had more than tea on her agenda. She fixed a canny eye on the newcomer and, having ascertained that he was married and had an eight-year-old daughter, led him to the nursery. When Keenan came back he was holding a rashy, blue-eyed baby. "Here," Sister Philomena said, producing a bottle, "you feed him."

Holding the child eased an ache the surgeon had carried a long time. He and his wife had lost several babies during their marriage—the last one, a boy, about a year before. Now, leaving, he promised, "I'll bring something for that rash."

He was back the next day with ointment. Then he sat down and began feeding baby George. "Tell me, doctor," Sister Philomena asked, "is it likely that you might want to adopt a little tyke like this one?"

"Yes, it's likely," Keenan said.

When he returned to the *Consolation*, he asked for his captain's advice.

"Lieutenant, your job is to take care of military personnel," the captain said. Keenan had to tell Sister Philomena that adopting George was out of the question. But he kept coming back to hold the baby.

Then came a long stretch when he couldn't get shore leave. When he finally got back to the orphanage Sister told him George was gone. Her friend, Chaplain Edward Riley, had received a passport for him and taken him to the *Point Cruz*. "He's going to send George to an orphanage in America."

"The hell he is!" Keenan yelled as he ran out.

When Father Riley carried "George Cruz Ascom" up the gangway of the *Point Cruz*, 1000 men lined the rail. For days, they had worked to prepare a nursery in the sick bay. Ship's carpenters had built a crib and playpen. Both were so full of homemade rattles and toys that there was barely room for George. A foot-high stack of diapers had been cut from Navy sheets and painstakingly hemmed in the ship's laundry.

The baby was put in the charge of two hospital corpsmen, both seasoned fathers. The flight surgeon, a pediatrician in civilian life, had the galley make special formula. Within days the listless, spindly infant began filling out and worming around in his crib.

So many men requested permission to visit the nursery that Captain Hayward instituted "Baby-san Call." After nap time each afternoon, the ship's public-address system would blare out: "Attention all hands! Baby-san on the hangar deck from 1400 hours!" Men would run for their cameras and file past the bomb cart that had become a baby carriage. They would coo at George and snap his picture. Some offered George a forefinger and he would curl his tiny fist around it and laugh.

"That baby had 1000 uncles," said William J. Powers, the petty officer in charge of the hangar deck. "By then, the armistice was signed and we were all waiting to go home, and along comes this little kid to hit us right in the heart. It was as though he was the peace we'd been fighting for."

George had been aboard the *Point Cruz* more than a week the day Lt. Hugh Keenan came stomping up the gangway looking for Father Riley. What did Father intend to do with the baby from Sister Philomena's orphanage?

Father Riley, stricken, assumed Keenan had been sent by naval authorities. He admitted they had a baby on board. They were looking for an orphanage in the States.

"What if I told you I wanted to adopt the baby?" Keenan said. Father Riley gasped. "I'd say God bless you, my son—he's yours!"

They embraced and went looking for Hayward. The captain fired questions at Keenan, but the young surgeon's answers were sensible. The three agreed that George would stay aboard the *Point Cruz*. Since Keenan still had a year to serve, Captain Hayward would try to arrange passage for George to the States.

When the news was announced to the crew at dinner that night, a cheer ripped through the mess.

Back on the *Consolation*, Hugh Keenan was struck by the numbing realization of what he had done. He went at once to the wardroom and wrote his wife. "I am making arrangements to send you a Christmas present that I hope you will love." The days crawled by as he waited for her reply. When it came, the envelope was fat and the letter was long, but the answer was: Yes!

Things were not going well for Father Riley. Korean nationals needed a visa to enter the United States, but when he applied for one, the U.S. consulate told him the quota was filled. Maybe next year.

As time passed, a visa for the baby seemed out of reach. Then, in mid-November, Hayward was invited to a dinner in Seoul where he was to receive a decoration. Vice President Nixon was also scheduled to attend. At the reception there was a good deal of talk about "Chick Hayward's baby"—every flag officer in Korea having heard the story by this time. An admiral friend of Hayward's told Nixon about George and his desperate need for a visa. Nixon turned to Ellis O. Brigg, the American ambassador in Seoul, and spoke the magic words: "Can you help out here?"

Seven days later, the visa came.

In late November, Lt. Hugh Keenan kissed his new son good-bye and handed him over to the crew of the *Point Cruz*, which was about to set sail for Japan. Several days later, "1000 uncles" cheered while the bosun's mate piped George Cruz Ascom, IBfc—Infant Boy, first class—over the side, and the baby was turned over to Father Riley, his escort to America via military transport ship.

The *Point Cruz* finally made it back to the United States in December 1953. Father Riley went on to Central America, where he served as a missionary until his death. Chick Hayward, the one-time high school dropout, became a vice admiral and, with the USS *Enterprise* as his flagship, became the first admiral to command a nuclear task force.

In America, George became Daniel Edward Keenan—Daniel for Hugh's father, Edward for Father Riley. Growing up in Spokane, where his father returned to practice general surgery, Danny dreamed of becoming a sportswriter. He graduated from Washington State University with a degree in communications in 1977. Today he's married and works as sports editor of the biweekly *Grant County Journal* in Ephrata, Washington, a town of 5300.

One by one, the men of the *Point Cruz* had returned to peacetime pursuits, raised families, made careers. Over the years, they lost track of each other, but they never stopped wondering about "their" baby.

Bill Powers, the former hangar-deck chief, had served 30 years in the Navy. He told his four children the story of the baby on the aircraft carrier, told it to his eight grandchildren, and he can hardly wait until his five great-grandchildren are old enough so he can tell it again.

When a reunion of the *Point Cruz* crew was organized for September 1993, Bill was determined to have "George" there. He telephoned Keenan repeatedly, and encouraged him to attend the gathering. "Son, I knew you when you had to be burped after you ate. You have to come!"

Once the word was out that "George" would be there, a special expectancy took hold of the veterans. *Our baby is coming!* The former sailors crowded around to meet a handsome, well-built man, his eyes now turned to brown.

"I would go to the sick bay just to see you," said Donald J. Houlihan, recalling those magic moments in the improvised nursery. "I held you in my arms," one said. "I changed your diapers," another added with a laugh.

On the last night of the reunion, Danny Keenan rose to bid the men farewell. *How do I thank them for saving my life?* he wondered. The faces he looked out upon from the podium where he stood were still strangers to him, but he was touched deeply.

And then the words came. "Without you good men, I wouldn't be here," Danny said quietly. "Not in this hotel, not in this country. And maybe not even on this earth."

The men of the *Point Cruz* were ordinary men. They had saved a life without asking for praise or thanks. And now, late in their lives, they could see that their long-ago act of kindness had been something of great importance.

For a moment no one spoke. There was really no need. As it had once been a long time ago on the *Point Cruz*, it was again: Danny Keenan was surrounded by an ocean of fatherly love.

★ ★ ★

Veterans of a Forgotten Victory

BY RALPH KINNEY BENNETT

On June 25, 1950, the morning the war started, Private First Class Leonard Korgie, 25, of Columbus, Nebraska, was sleeping the deep, easy sleep of the men in the U.S. Eighth Army. For the victorious occupation forces in Japan, it was a life in which training was nil and "light duty" was often the order of the day.

Just over 650 miles to the northwest, the sky filled with flashes and thunderous concussions as North Korean artillery began a savage bombardment. Soon more than 90,000 North Koreans, supported by Soviet-built tanks, were streaming across the 38th Parallel separating North from South Korea. Within days, poorly trained South Korean troops were in panicky retreat.

President Truman committed U.S. forces to a "police action." The United Nations Security Council called on member states to help South Korea resist aggression.

Private Korgie was to be shipped to Korea on July 8. "Wow, we're going to fight!" he shouted to a buddy. Korgie had not fired a rifle in two years; he'd never thrown a grenade. He packed his summer dress uniform to wear in the victory parade his officers told him would probably take place within a few weeks.

When those few weeks had passed, Korgie was dirty, hungry, weakened by raging dysentery and longing for a few hours of peaceful sleep. He had seen men's stomachs laid open by mortar shells and a soldier next to him bayoneted to death. His regiment, the 34th Infantry, had 1981 men when it went into combat. Eight weeks later only 184 of them were left.

The fighting moved up the peninsula as the North Koreans were pushed clear to the Yalu River border with China. Then it moved back as hundreds of thousands of communist Chinese troops entered the war in November 1950.

Korgie will never forget the choking heat of the Korean summer and the vicious cold of the winter of 1950-51, when temperatures dropped to 20 below. He still remembers the sound of bodies being crushed as refugees fled over a Han River pontoon bridge at the same time as an armored column. And seared in his mind is the day his unit came upon an advance element of the Eighth Army, which had been massacred, then doused with gasoline and set afire.

Back home, with "absolutely no fear of anything anymore," Korgie was disappointed at people's indifference to the faraway war. Restless, he worked for a while in Denver and there met Jean DeMichelis, a vacationing schoolteacher from Rockford, Illinois. They were married in 1953.

This past May, Leonard and Jean Korgie retired after long careers in the Peoria, Illinois, public schools. Their two daughters have grown up and moved away. A son died of viral pneumonia in 1975.

Occasionally, Korgie is visited by a recurring nightmare—North Korean soldiers burst through his bedroom door, and he screams for someone to shoot them. Jean gently shakes him awake.

Sometimes when he's about to gripe about something, Korgie thinks of Korea and says, "Hell, this is nothing." And at veterans' reunions, when they blow taps in memory of dead comrades, he swallows hard and finds something stuck in his eye.

For Marine Sergeant Frank Takeyama, the whole of existence came down to a ragged horizon and the sky above it, a frozen moment when fear and death are put in perspective. In that tiny piece of sky, an object little bigger than a soup can tumbled lazily toward him.

"Grenade!" he yelled as he hit the dirt. But the blast caught him, and fragments tore bloody holes in his chest.

Stunned, yet amazingly calm, Takeyama walked off the hill. After 18 days in an aid station, he returned to dodging grenades on more hills. The men of Baker Company's First Platoon were glad to have him back. They knew him as a quiet, reliable leader with steely nerves, but they had no idea of the route he had traveled to fight for his country.

It was a journey begun five years earlier in a World War II internment camp for Japanese-Americans in California. His family was *sansei*, third-generation American, but they were interned nonetheless.

Takeyama was allowed to leave the camp to work as a houseboy for a Pasadena family while finishing his senior year in high school. The family's son, a career Marine, greatly impressed him and in 1946 Takeyama signed up for a two-year hitch. After that, he was in the reserves, attending college as a prelaw student.

When war broke out in Korea, Takeyama was less than three months from his discharge. Then President Truman extended enlistments one year. Takeyama got married on Thanksgiving Day, but he and his wife, Fumiko, had a short honeymoon. The following week he left for cold-weather training, and then Korea.

In August 1951, when he had long lost count of the hills he had assaulted, he was shipped home. After all the mud and heat and cold and filth and fear, "All I wanted to do was take hot showers, drink milk and eat green vegetables."

Today he and Fumiko live in Torrance, California, where he works for an aerospace firm. Their five children are grown, three with their own families.

Every month or so Takeyama gets together with some old Baker Company buddies for lunch. They talk more about their health and grandchildren than the dry-mouth nights and bloody days of 40 years ago.

But sometimes Frank Takeyama remembers rare, peaceful evenings when deep shadows hid the scars of war on the earth, and he looked across purple hills with the waning light reflected in the rice paddies. He felt South Korea was a beautiful place that deserved peace. "We were right to be there," he says quietly. "They're free, and we helped."

Luther Weaver, a short, unassuming man from Jackson, Georgia, had fought the Germans all the way across France with the 319th Infantry Regiment in 1944-45. He came home with a battlefield commission as second lieutenant, shrapnel scars on his face and the sound of artillery still pounding in his ears.

Weaver was a property officer for Georgia reserve units when Korea broke out. By September 1950 he was back in combat. Soon promoted to captain, he took command of Love Company, 35th Infantry Regiment, not long after the men had come through the devastating and demoralizing retreat from the Yalu River in sub-zero weather. Weaver was their fourth commander in less than two months. His predecessors had spent most of their time in the command post. The first night Weavers troops came under attack, they were surprised to find him among them, coolly directing the defense. The men marveled that the "Old Man" could move so fast on such short legs.

Weaver led Love Company through battle after battle. Then in June 1951, after almost 600 days in combat in two wars, he was posted to battalion headquarters.

The relative calm for Weaver was short-lived. Having traveled with relief troops to visit his old company one night in early September, he found himself in the middle of an attack on their hill position. Weaver grabbed an old shotgun and brought down three communist soldiers before it jammed. He fought with his pistol until daybreak, when the Chinese finally broke off the attack.

Weaver began organizing litter teams and walking wounded. Getting them under cover in a valley below, he heard reports of many more wounded on the hill. Returning at dusk to search for them, he ran into a Chinese patrol.

Weaver spent a night eluding the Chinese, then made his way through a minefield back inside his lines. The next day he watched as the bodies of his comrades from Love Company were brought off the hill. "I had known these men," he says, "known them by their first names."

Weaver stayed in the Army and retired as a lieutenant colonel. He hunts, fishes and lives quietly with his wife in Macon, Georgia. Of all his citations and mementos, Weaver treasures most a handwritten letter dated June 1951. It is from the men of Love Company thanking the "Old Man" for being "the best damned commander in the U.S. Army."

War was the last thing on his mind when Victor Fox, 17, joined the peacetime Army in 1949. A year later, as the Canadian-born Detroiter's troopship sailed out from Oakland past Alcatraz, prisoners shouted from the yard, "You'll be sorry!"

Fox was assigned to Item Company, which was ordered to assault Hill 174. He found himself charging the hill with fixed bayonet as grenades and mortar shells exploded around him. All night he threw grenades at the enemy while his buddy Bill Haltom batted incoming ones away. North Korean bodies piled up around their position. By the second day, Fox could eat his rations nonchalandy under the grotesque stares of the corpses.

When Item was driven off the hill, Fox stumbled down a creek bed dragging a wounded GI. Later, near a stone wall, he sensed a rush of air and a flash of light, and then nothing. He came to on a stretcher. Dazed and not sure of the extent of his wounds, Fox got up and returned to duty. He took part in another assault on Hill 174 the next day before he was taken to an aid station and treated for shrapnel wounds.

Fox would battle up and down the Korean peninsula with

Item Company. He fought in Chipyong-ni, the battle in which American firepower ended the myth of Chinese invincibility. But Hill 174 would stay with him more than anything else.

When Fox came home, he tried school and held various factory jobs around Chicago for 14 years before moving with his wife, Lillian, to San Francisco. Today, he works as a night auditor for an athletic club.

Fox had pretty much put aside all thoughts of Korea until he was asked to contribute to Donald Knox's *The Korean War: An Oral History*. Reflecting on those years, Fox says, "I don't regret one minute of it. We went to help the Korean people, and we did it."

He is not the kind of man to keep reliving the war. But sometimes if he's walking outside on a rainy day, automobile tires hissing on the wet pavement sound like an incoming mortar round, and he winces.

Patrick T. "Paddy" McGahn, Jr., graduated from Mt. Saint Mary's College in Emmitsburg, Maryland, in June 1950 with a reserve commission as a Marine second lieutenant. He planned to go to law school in the fall. He was enjoying his last summer along Atlantic City's boardwalk when he heard about Korea. "I had to study a map to see where it was."

Called to active duty, McGahn arrived in Korea in March 1951 and within three weeks was wounded by mortar fire. Then, on the night of April 22, he led a platoon up a ridge vital to the protection of the 1st Marine Division's right flank near the town of Hwachon.

Ten yards from the ridge line a grenade exploded, tearing

into his face. Moments later he was grazed by machine-gun fire. When he turned to see if his men were still with him, an enemy soldier fired a burst that hit him in the back of the head. McGahn refused to be treated until the rest of his men had received attention. The platoon held the hill, and he was evacuated to a hospital.

McGahn returned to his unit May 9. Within a week, he was wounded again by mortar fragments. He stayed on the line. Two weeks after that, an enemy grenade went off near his feet, and he felt something pierce his back. He kept fighting for another five days, wondering why his back hurt so much. There were shell fragments near his spine.

McGahn was sent back to the United States, where he would spend the next six months in military hospitals. After only three months in Korea, he had won four Purple Hearts, the Navy Cross and the Bronze Star Medal.

Today, McGahn is a successful lawyer in New Jersey. You can see the scars on his face and the "railroad tracks" made by bullets on the back of his head. He shakes your hand with his left. He's gradually losing the use of the right, because of the damage to his spine.

Public indifference to returning veterans had bothered McGahn for a long time. Last year he did something about it. When Marine veterans gathered in Atlantic City, McGahn arranged for the Marine Band to come up from Quantico, Virginia. It assembled on the dock while the veterans were on a cruise. When they returned, the band was playing "The Marine's Hymn" to greet them. Paddy McGahn cried. Everybody cried.

The Long Way Home

BY JOHN G. HUBBELL

"Kaylor," said the lieutenant, "tomorrow morning at 0600, when the Regiment moves up, you report to S-I. Your dependency discharge has come through and you're going back to Casual Company at Hamhung."

Bud Kaylor, Marine machine gunner, was stunned, then elated. This was no foxhole rumor, this was for real. He was getting out of this frozen hell and going home. He'd be there in time for Christmas with his wife, Dorothy, and their family.

Early the next morning, Kaylor said quick good-byes to his buddies. The First Marine Division and the Army's Seventh Infantry were moving north for an assault on the Chosin Reservoir. But for Bud Kaylor the war was over, or so he thought. This, however, was the morning of November 28, 1950, and no one knew that the stage was set for the attack by the Chinese Reds.

At S-I the personnel officer told Kaylor he'd have to get back to Hamhung on his own. So he and Art Foley, a mail clerk, hitched a ride in the lead truck of a five-truck convoy. There were two other Marine passengers in the back of their truck, and another riding shotgun with the driver. Thus Bud Kaylor started the first leg of his journey out of Korea, and home.

The home he was headed for was near Hopkins, Minnesota, where Gladys and Charley Kaylor, Bud's parents, live. It was there that the telegram was to arrive on January 5, 1951. It came from Marine Headquarters, with deep regrets: Pfc. Charles Martin Kaylor had been missing in action since November 28, 1950.

"The telegram said 'missing,'" Charley Kaylor relates. "Bud is a little guy, but he's tough, cool and a quick thinker. He had always been an athlete. I figured he was still alive somewhere."

Neither could Bud's wife or his mother or his sisters give up. His daughter, Terry Jo, was only four, but she was sure her father would come back. Through the long months that followed, they all lived on the strength of interminable prayer and desperate hope.

Soon after Kavlor's convoy got underway that morning for the 70-mile trip, they came to a small village. The huts looked uninhabited, but in seconds a crowd of Koreans was streaming out. They shouted and pointed down the road.

"Poor gooks think the Commies are coming back," someone said.

The Marines waved and laughed, and some threw candy and cigarettes. Soon they found out what the Koreans had been trying to tell them. Around a sharp bend they came on a jeep in the middle of the road, with logs piled high on either side of it. The driver of the lead truck couldn't avoid hitting it. The jeep rolled off the road and the driver bulled his way on.

Bud Kaylor looked over the edge of the truck. Chinese soldiers were six and seven deep in the ditches, and more were running down the hills on both sides of the road, shooting as they came. Kaylor grabbed his carbine and emptied it into one of the ditches. There wasn't time to aim, and the Reds were so thick it didn't make any difference.

In a matter of seconds his ammunition was gone. He dropped flat on his back and saw two bullets sing past, within an inch of his nose. He saw them go by, because they had come right through the steel side of the truck, and it had slowed them down. Then one came through and got Art Foley, the mail clerk. Kaylor started to reach for Art's carbine, and he saw something yellow sail by. It was a grenade shaped like a potato masher and he leaped for it, but it wasn't there so he thought it had bounced out of the truck. But when he lay down again his head hit something hard; he reached back and grabbed it. It was the grenade. He threw it backward, over his head, and heard it go off.

A minute later the driver was shot in the ear. The Marine riding shotgun with him kept firing at the ditch on the driver's side of the road, trying to protect him. There were only two tires left, and the truck veered all over the road.

Kaylor grabbed Foley's carbine and sat up at the back of the truck. He was just in time to see a Red soldier lob one of those yellow grenades up from the ditch. It was a perfect throw, and Kaylor grabbed it by the handle and slammed it right back at him. It hit at his feet and went off. The Red died with unbelieving surprise on his face.

Then the truck went off the road into the ditch. Kaylor went over the side and ran to some thin bushes. From there he could see the truck driver and his gunner running toward a frozen river about 500 yards away. The Reds shot at them from a hill and Kaylor watched the bullets kick up the snow around their feet. Suddenly the gunner dropped, but the driver kept right on going across the river, into thick woods.

A number of Reds showed up, and one threw a grenade that landed about five feet from Kaylor. It went off and knocked him down, and he was conscious of a burning sensation in his leg.

The Reds came up and stood all around him, looking at him and pointing their rifles. Then one moved in close and frisked him.

Kaylor saw the red stain come through his pant leg. The blood was running fast. His captors took him to a command post where an officer called two orderlies over and gave them some instructions. Then he turned to Kaylor and made him take his parka off. He pretended that he was searching it, and he motioned to the orderlies to take Kaylor away. As Kaylor left he saw the officer trying on his parka.

Bud was weak from loss of blood. He kept falling down, and the Reds kept pushing him along. Every step seemed colder than the last. It was 15 degrees below zero, and all Kaylor wore now was his field cap, a shirt, pants, shoes, and long underwear. At a battalion aid station, the Red orderlies dressed his wounds.

Early the second morning, when they reached a Korean village, one of the Reds walked Kaylor to the door of a house and motioned him inside. Entering, Bud could see three Chinese officers at a table. A single candle illuminated the entire room. In a few seconds another officer came in. He was young and friendly, and his English was flawless. He put out his hand and smiled.

"I'm Lieutenant Fung," he said. "Won't you sit down?"

Fung asked his name, rate and serial number. He translated swiftly to the three officers at the table. Then he asked Kaylor the names of Marine officers in his outfit, how many tanks were there, and what kind of artillery. Kaylor started to say that he wasn't required to tell, when he felt a sharp kick at his leg. He looked around, and at the end of the bench he saw two Chinese overcoats piled over a body, with only the feet showing. Kaylor moved farther down the bench, away from the body, and told the lieutenant he couldn't answer him.

In a few minutes Fung left the room, and the body under the overcoats sat up and unveiled itself. It was the truck driver, 19-year-old Cpl. Fred Holcomb, from Hamden, New York, and he was more than a little indignant at having been captured, and all the Chinamen in Korea could go to hell.

"We don't tell them a thing," he said. "We don't have to."

Kaylor was sorry that Holcomb hadn't escaped, but glad he was finally in good Marine company. They started talking about the ambush, and then Fung came back into the room. He talked to the two Marines until dawn. He explained that the Chinese were not going to kill them, that they didn't even want them as prisoners.

"All we want to do with you guys," he said, "is get you out of Korea so you can't fight us any more." He said they were going to take them to China, put them on a neutral ship, and send them back to the United States. Then he took their home addresses.

"I'd like to write you fellows after the war and see how things turn out for each of us," he said. He told them they would be moving out in the morning, shook hands and said good-bye. And he left them with the memory of a warm and friendly person.

It was snowing heavily when they moved out with a Chinese column and started walking north. After four days they joined a group of 250 other prisoners, including 43 Marines. They moved on north, Kaylor limping along on his wounded leg over the icy mountain trails. And finally, after they had walked for 11 days, and just when Bud thought he couldn't walk another mile, they stopped moving. They were in the village of Kang-gye, near the Yalu River.

The Chinese divided them into two sections and billeted them in cold Korean houses, where most of them lay on the bare floor in a sleeping stupor for days. When they were strong enough to want to stop sleeping, the Chinese took their clothes and gave them Chinese uniforms. English-speaking Red officers began to interrogate them. It was kept mostly on a personal plane, and the officers kept it up until they got the answers they wanted. If Comrade Kaylor, for instance, said he earned $250 a month at his job in Minneapolis, he was obviously lying. This made the Chinese angry, and they would spend long hours explaining to him that he was among friends and there was no need for him to lie. Patiently, they would point out to him that his warmongering, capitalistic bosses on Wall Street had duped him into thinking he was well off.

When the prisoners realized what the Reds wanted to hear, they told them tales of wretched, hungry childhoods that had been lived in anticipation of joining the Marine Corps, where they could at least get some food and clothing. They told of aged parents who lived as best they could on the infrequent and niggardly charity of the Wall Street bosses. The Chinese seemed to like this.

The indoctrination began in a bleak, cold barn called the Big House. A Chinese "high commander" came out on a stage and made a welcoming speech. They were not, he explained, to think of themselves as prisoners. They were "newly liberated friends," and would be treated as such. The Chinese people were not angry with them for being in Korea, since they had been duped by their imperialistic bosses. They would be treated with kindness, but they must obey the rules set down for newly liberated friends. If they broke the rules they would undergo severe punishment.

On Christmas night all the newly liberated friends were herded into the Big House. The Chinese had decorated the place with Christmas trees and candles, wreaths and red paper bells. There was a big sign saying, "Merry Christmas." Along the walls were signs reading, "If it were not for the Wall Street imperialists, you would be home with your wives and families this Christmas night." A high commander made a speech that repeated what the signs said, and he threw in a few unkind remarks about Truman, MacArthur, and Dulles.

By this time the POWs knew what the Chinese wanted of them, and word had spread that the "most promising" prisoners would be released before the war was over. So after the high commander finished speaking, a Marine from Boston named McClean jumped up and shouted, "Down with the Wall Street bosses!" And another named Dickerson pulled his six feet seven inches from the floor and shouted in a Georgia drawl, "Down with the aggressive imperialists!" And a five-foot nine-inch Marine named Kaylor limped over to a toothy interpreter named Lieutenant Pan, looked him squarely in the eye, and cried, "Down with the warmongers!" The newly liberated friends all over the Big House took up the cry, and the happy, smiling Chinese ran around the huge room, patting them on the back and shaking hands with them and giving them presents. Each man received ten pieces of candy, six cigarettes and a Christmas card.

After Christmas each section was lectured every other day in the Big House. They listened to long orations by high commanders of varying stature. Sometimes the teachers spoke in Chinese, and this took the longest because an interpreter had to translate it. Sometimes they would rattle along in a high-pitched, singsong English. First, they spoke on "Why Are We Treating You So Well?" Then, "Who Is the Aggressor in Korea?" Then, "Why Is the United States the Aggressor?" Then, "How You Can Fight for Peace."

After the lectures the section marched back to its house, where it would engage in a roundtable discussion. An English-speaking Chinese officer would sit quietly by, listening and taking notes. Once in a while he would inject a comment, and the Marines would all nod solemn approval.

The weeks stretched into months, and the pattern became routine.

And then dysentery hit. It hit everyone, and the ones it hit the worst died. Sometimes only one would die in a week, sometimes three or five.

Worse than the dysentery was the malnutrition; they had nothing to eat but sorghum seed and millet. Malnutrition hit the legs with a screaming viciousness. When it hit Kaylor he lay flat on his back for 28 days and cried and became delirious, while agonizing pains raced through his legs. When it would stop for a while, he would drift off to sleep, and suddenly wake up screaming when the pains came back. Then, after days of this, exhaustion would claim him, and the pain would lie dormant while he slept. Finally his legs felt better and he was able to move around again.

It was March now, and the days got longer and warmer. And the rumors got thicker that some of the most "promising" friends were soon to be released. The combination kept the prisoners in anxious good spirits. But it was with some reluctance that every man in the camp signed the Stockholm Peace Petition. The Chinese thought it would be a good indication of their sincerity in their desire to fight for peace. The Marines hoped that the names might somehow sift back through the oblivion they had walked into and reach the United States.

And on March 21 the second telegram arrived at the house of Charley Kaylor in Hopkins, Minnesota. The message was from the Army's Provost Marshal General, and it said that the name of Charles Martin Kaylor had been mentioned on an enemy propaganda broadcast out of Peking on March 16. That's all it said. But now the constant, desperate hope became a fire.

On Easter Sunday 60 prisoners were herded into the Big House. Inside, great care was taken to seat a certain 30 on one side of the room, and the rest on the other side. Then a high commander delivered a lengthy singsong reiteration of all the lectures of the months before. He climaxed this oration with the news that one of these groups of 30 was to be released. It was felt, he said, that these men were "ready to carry on the fight for peace among their own people." The other 30 were being cited for "progress," but were being kept for a while to help instruct incoming newly liberated friends. Then he smiled and toyed with these 60 men.

"Which group is it?" he asked. "Who is going home? Is it the group on my right? Or is it the group on my left?" Bud Kaylor looked around at the faces in his group. Harrison, Estess, Dickerson, Holcomb, Maffioli—all were barracks bull-session artists, and all had given the Reds master snow jobs.

Finally the high commander pointed to the group on his right. It was Kaylor's group. "This group," he said, "leaves tonight." The 30 Marines took the news with stone-faced joy, for they wanted the Reds to feel they would just as soon stay there and be Communists as go home and be Communists. The other 30 also remained stone-faced, but they had trouble fighting back the tears.

The prisoners to be released moved out in trucks at dusk and rode for five nights. On the fifth night Lieutenant Pan, the interpreter in command, got them out of the trucks and told them they were in the Chunchon area.

"There has been an American offensive," he said. "It is too dangerous to let you go now. You might be killed."

The Marines said they would take that chance, but Pan told them he was acting under orders. Then the trucks moved away and the Marines were marched to a prison camp.

They stayed in this camp six weeks. Then, on the night of May 15, the Chinese called out 19 of the 30 Marines and marched them to a river. They gave them razors and soap, and let them bathe and shave, then brought them chow. The food was pork and rice, and it was the first time in six months that any of them had seen anything but sorghum seed and millet. A lot of them ate too much too fast and got sick. Bud Kaylor was one of them. After they finished eating, Lieutenant Pan spoke to them.

"Word has come from the high command to release you men," he said.

Again they were loaded into trucks. On the third night they reached the Imjin River. Retreating Chinese troops were coming back across the river by the thousands. Pan turned his charges over to a field commander. The commander told them that another offensive had been started and they could not be released at this time. Then he left, saying he would be back about midnight and for them to be ready to move back up north.

T/Sgt. Charley Harrison, of Tulsa, Oklahoma, was fighting mad. He announced firmly that he was not going up north again. He was going home, and if anyone wanted to come with him they were welcome.

U.N. artillery was whistling in close, and the guards were in foxholes. So all 19 Marines sneaked off and waded across the shallow Imjin River. On the other side they ran for miles through the woods.

Just before dawn they stopped in a field where the wheat was high, and went to sleep. They awoke to find four Chinese soldiers pointing their guns at them and jabbering to each other. Then Harrison, who spoke Chinese, put on an act. He got up smiling. He explained that they were released prisoners of war and that the high command would be displeased if they were shot or taken back. The Chinese jabbered back at him, and then he talked some more. And then he started talking to the Marines out of the side of his mouth.

"These birds aren't going to let us go," he said. "They're arguing whether they should shoot us now or take us in." Then he said something in Chinese. Then he spoke English again. "Estess and Dickerson get the one on the left." More Chinese. "Kaylor and Hilburn the one on the right, Nash and Holcomb the one next to him." More Chinese. "Hawkins and Hay ton the other one." Then there was more Chinese, and finally Harrison gave the word: "Let's get 'em!"

The Marines did their jobs as Harrison assigned them, and completed them quickly when the others pitched in. This was a kill-or-be-killed situation. The Marines overpowered the Reds and strangled them and smashed their heads with the gun butts. Then they ran.

In the next valley they came to a village. A bearded old Korean sent them up to a house on the top of a hill, where the mayor used to live, and promised to send them food and tobacco. They were to wait there until he could send a message to the American troops, who were only a few miles away.

Inside the house they lay and marveled that this was the only house any of them had seen in Korea with wallpaper. And then they heard the sound of an airplane. They looked outside and saw an L-5 artillery observer, an Army plane, flying low. They quickly cut the wallpaper into strips and took it out to the rice paddy behind the house. They spelled out POW 19 RESCUE, and then they went back inside. Only Fred Holcomb stayed out in the rice paddy, waving his undershirt to attract the L-5's attention. Snipers fired at him from the hills occasionally, but they weren't coming close, and Holcomb was too excited to care.

Soon Holcomb came running in. The L-5 had dropped a message: "Come out to the letters and be counted. We are sending tanks in to pick you up."

They went back to the letters and in half an hour they saw the L-5 leading three tanks around a bend in the draw that stretched out beneath the rice paddies. Then Lt. Frank Cold, of Tampa, Florida, the only officer among these 19, lined them up in a column of twos.

"I know how we all feel about being rescued," he said. "But this is the Army coming in to get us, and we're still Marines. So let's be rescued like Marines, in formation."

The tanks stopped about 300 yards from them to identify them, and this was hard to do since they wore Chinese uniforms. But finally they moved up close and the hatch of the lead tank opened. An Army captain came out of it.

The 19 Marines stood there, in columns of twos, in a soggy, worthless no man's land, somewhere in Korea, and tears as big as raindrops streamed down the face of every one of them. The Army captain stood looking at them, and for a moment it seemed as though all Korea was silent. Then the captain said, "Come on, fellas, let's get the hell out of here!" So they climbed into the tanks and got the hell out of there, but they were rescued like Marines.

It was on May 25 that the third telegram arrived at Charley Kaylor's house. It came from Marine Headquarters, and it said that Pfc. Charles Martin Kaylor would soon be home. The end-less months of hoping and praying were over, and the miracle had happened. But the people in Charley Kaylor's house said one more prayer anyhow.

Then, almost suddenly, it was June 23, and Bud Kaylor was moving down the steps from the airplane, while his eyes searched the faces at the end of the ramp. Then he saw them, right in front, smiling and waving. He limped toward them. Then Dorothy was in his arms, the others clustered around. Bud Kaylor had come the long way home from Korea.

THE VIETNAM WAR

★ ★ ★

The Courage of Sam Bird

BY B. T. COLLINS

I met Capt. Samuel R. Bird on a dusty road near An Khe, South Vietnam, one hot July day in 1966. I was an artillery forward observer with Bravo Company, 2nd/12th Cavalry, 1st Cavalry Division, and I looked it. I was filthy, sweaty, and jaded by war, and I thought, *Oh, brother, get a load of this.* Dressed in crisply starched fatigues, Captain Bird was what we called "squared away"—ramrod straight, eyes on the horizon. Hell, you could still see the shine on his boot tips beneath the road dust.

After graduation from Officer Candidate School, I had sought adventure by volunteering for Vietnam. But by that hot and dangerous July, I was overdosed on "adventure," keenly interested in survival and very fond of large rocks and deep holes. Bird was my fourth company commander, and my expectations were somewhat cynical when he called all his officers and sergeants together.

"I understand this company has been in Vietnam almost a year and has never had a party," he said. Now, we officers and sergeants had our little clubs to which we repaired. So we stole bewildered looks at one another, cleared our throats and wondered what this wiry newcomer was talking about. "The men are going to have a party," he announced, "and they're not going to pay for it. Do I make myself clear?"

A party for the "grunts" was the first order of business! Sam Bird had indeed made himself clear. We all chipped in to get food and beer for about 160 men. The troops were surprised almost to the point of suspicion—who, after all, had ever done anything for them? But that little beer and bull session was exactly what those war-weary men needed. Its effect on morale was profound. I began to watch our new captain more closely.

Bird and I were the same age, 26, but eons apart in everything else. He was from the sunny heartland of Kansas, I from the suburbs of New York City. He prayed every day and was close to his God. My faith had evaporated somewhere this side of altar boy. I was a college dropout who had wandered into the Army with the words "discipline problem" close on my heels. He had graduated from The Citadel, South Carolina's proud old military school.

If ever a man looked like a leader, it was Sam Bird. He was tall and lean, with penetrating blue eyes. But the tedium and terror of a combat zone take far sterner qualities than mere appearance.

Our outfit was helicoptered to a mountain outpost one day for the thankless task of preparing a position for others to occupy. We dug trenches, filled sandbags, strung wire under a blistering sun. It was hard work, and Sam was everywhere, pitching in with the men. A colonel who was supposed to oversee the operation remained at a shelter, doing paperwork. Sam looked at what his troops had accomplished, then, red-faced, strode over to the colonel's sanctuary. We couldn't hear what he was saying to his superior, but we had the unmistakable sense that Sam was uncoiling a bit. The colonel suddenly found time to inspect the fortifications and thank the men for a job well done.

Another day, this time on the front lines after weeks of awful chow, we were given something called "coffee cake" that had the look and texture of asphalt paving. Furious, Sam got on the radio phone to headquarters. He reached the colonel and said, "Sir, you and the supply officer need to come out here and taste the food, because this rifle company is not taking one step further." Not a good way to move up in the Army, I thought. But the colonel came out, and the food improved from that moment. Such incidents were not lost on the men of Bravo Company.

During the monsoon season we had to occupy a landing zone. The torrential, wind-driven rains had been falling for weeks. Like everyone else I sat under my poncho in a stupor, wondering how much of the wetness was rainwater and how much was sweat. Nobody cared that the position was becoming flooded. We had all just crawled inside ourselves. Suddenly I saw Sam, Mr. Spit and Polish, with nothing on but his olive-drab undershorts and his boots. He was digging a drainage ditch down the center of the camp. He didn't say anything, just dug away, mud spattering his chest, steam rising from his back and shoulders. Slowly and sheepishly we emerged from under our ponchos, and shovels in hand, we began helping "the old man" get the ditch dug. We got the camp tolerably dried out and with that one simple act transformed our morale.

Sam deeply loved the U.S. Army, its history and traditions. Few of the men knew it, but he had been in charge of a special honors unit of the Old Guard, which serves at the Tomb of the Unknown Soldier in Arlington National Cemetery and participates in the Army's most solemn ceremonies. He was the kind of guy whose eyes would mist during the singing of the National Anthem.

Sam figured patriotism was just a natural part of being an American. But he knew that morale was a function not so much of inspiration as of good boots, dry socks, extra ammo and hot meals.

Sam's philosophy was to put his troops first. On that foundation he built respect a brick at a time. His men ate first; he ate last. Instead of merely learning their names, he made it a point to know the men. A lot of the soldiers were high-school dropouts and would-be tough guys just a few years younger than himself. Some were scared, and a few were still in partial shock at being in a shooting war. Sam patiently worked on their pride and self-confidence. Yet there was never any doubt who was in charge. I had been around enough to know what a delicate accomplishment that was.

Half in wonder, an officer once told me, "Sam can dress a

man down till his ears burn, and the next minute that same guy is eager to follow him into hell." But he never chewed out a man in front of his subordinates.

Sam wouldn't ask his men to do anything he wasn't willing to do himself. He dug his own foxholes. He never gave lectures on appearance, but even at Godforsaken outposts in the Central Highlands, he would set aside a few ounces of water from his canteen to shave. His uniform, even if it was jungle fatigues, would be as clean and neat as he could make it. Soon all of Bravo Company had a reputation for looking sharp.

One sultry and miserable day on a dirt road at the base camp, Sam gathered the men together and began talking about how tough the infantryman's job is, how proud he was of them, how they should always look out for each other. He took out a bunch of Combat Infantryman's Badges, signifying that a soldier has paid his dues under fire, and he presented one to each of the men. There wasn't a soldier there who would have traded that moment on the road for some parade ground ceremony.

That was the way Sam Bird taught me leadership. He packed a lot of lessons into the six months we served together: Put the troops first. Know that morale often depends on small things. Respect every persons dignity. Always be ready to fight for your people. Lead by example. Reward performance. But Sam had another lesson to teach, one that would take long and painful years, a lesson in courage.

I left Bravo Company in December 1966 to return to the States for a month before joining a Special Forces unit. Being a big, tough paratrooper, I didn't tell Sam what his example had meant to me. But I made a point of visiting his parents and sister in Wichita, Kansas, just before Christmas to tell them how much he'd affected my life, and how his troops would walk off a cliff for him. His family was relieved when I told them that his tour of combat was almost over and he'd be moving to a safe job in the rear.

Two months later, in a thatched hut in the Mekong Delta, I got a letter from Sam's sister, saying that he had conned his commanding officer into letting him stay an extra month with his beloved Bravo Company. On his last day, January 27, 1967—his 27th birthday—the men had secretly planned a party, even arranging to have a cake flown in. They were going to "pay back the old man." But orders came down for Bravo to lead an airborne assault on a North Vietnamese regimental headquarters.

Sam's helicopter was about to touch down at the attack point when it was ripped by enemy fire. Slugs shattered his left ankle and right leg. Another struck the left side of his head, carrying off almost a quarter of his skull. His executive officer, Lt. Dean Parker, scooped Sam's brains back into the gaping wound.

Reading the letter, I felt as if I'd been kicked in the stomach. I began querying every hospital in Vietnam to find out if Sam was still alive. But in June, before I could discover his fate, I was in a firefight in an enemy-controlled zone. I had thrown four grenades. The fifth one exploded in my hand. I lost an arm and a leg.

Nearly a year later, in March 1968, I finally caught up with

Sam. I was just getting the hang of walking with an artificial leg when I visited him at the VA Medical Center in Memphis, Tennessee. Seeing him, I had to fight back the tears. The wiry, smiling soldier's soldier was blind in the left eye and partially so in the right. Surgeons had removed metal shards and damaged tissue from deep within his brain, and he had been left with a marked depression on the left side of his head. The circles under his eyes told of sleepless hours and great pain.

The old clear voice of command was slower now, labored and with an odd, high pitch. I saw his brow knit as he looked through his one good eye, trying to remember. He recognized me, but believed I had served with him in Korea, his first tour of duty.

Slowly, Sam rebuilt his ability to converse. But while he could recall things from long ago, he couldn't remember what he had eaten for breakfast. Headaches came on him like terrible firestorms. There was pain, too, in his legs. He had only partial use of one arm, with which he'd raise himself in front of the mirror to brush his teeth and shave.

He had the support of a wonderful family, and once he was home in Wichita, his sister brought his old school sweetheart, Annette Blazier, to see him. A courtship began, and in 1972 they married.

They built a house like Sam had dreamed of—red brick, with a flagpole out front. He had developed the habit of addressing God as "Sir" and spoke to him often. He never asked to be healed. At every table grace, he thanked God for sending him Annette and for "making it possible for me to live at home in a free country."

In 1976, Sam and Annette traveled to The Citadel for his 15th class reunion. World War II hero Gen. Mark Clark, the school's president emeritus, asked about his wounds and said, "On behalf of your country, I want to thank you for all you did."

With pride, Sam answered, "Sir, it was the least I could do."

Later Annette chided him gently for understating the case. After all, he had sacrificed his health and career in Vietnam. Sam gave her an incredulous look. "I had friends who didn't come back," he said. "I'm enjoying the freedoms they died for."

I visited Sam in Wichita and phoned him regularly. You would not have guessed that he lived with pain every day. Once, speaking of me to his sister, he said, "I should never complain about the pain in my leg, because B.T. doesn't have a leg." I'd seen a lot of men with lesser wounds reduced to anger and self-pity. Never a hint of that passed Sam's lips, though I knew that, every waking moment, he was fighting to live.

On October 18, 1984, after 17 years, Sam's body couldn't take any more. When we received the news of his death, a number of us from Bravo Company flew to Wichita, where Sam was to be buried with his forebears.

The day before the burial, his old exec, Dean Parker, and I went to the funeral home to make sure everything was in order. As Dean straightened the brass on Sam's uniform, I held my captain's hand and looked into his face, a face no longer filled with pain. I thought about how unashamed Sam always was to express his love for his country, how sunny and unaffected he was in his devotion to his men. I ached that I had never told him what a fine soldier and man he was. But in my deep sadness I felt a glow of pride for having served with him, and for having learned the lessons of leadership that would serve me all my life. That is why I am telling you about Samuel R. Bird and these things that happened so long ago.

Chances are, you have seen Sam Bird. He was the tall officer in charge of the casket detail at the funeral of President John F. Kennedy. Historian William Manchester described him as "a lean, sinewy Kansan, the kind of American youth whom Congressmen dutifully praise each Fourth of July and whose existence many, grown jaded by years on the Hill, secretly doubt."

There can be no doubt about Sam, about who he was, how he lived and how he led. We buried him that fall afternoon, as they say, "with honors." But as I walked from that grave, I knew I was the honored one, for having known him.

★ ★ ★

Submarines to the Rescue!

BY RALPH SEELEY WITH ALLEN RANKIN

We were loafing southward toward Guam on the afternoon of July 8, 1972, the periscope of our black, 300-foot nuclear submarine, the USS *Gurnard*, cleaving gentle waves. Suddenly I felt the sub dive, change course and throb with the strain of "Ahead flank," maximum forward speed. I groaned. After 63 days and nights submerged, on maneuvers, all of us aboard—I was an electrician's mate—were looking forward to shore leave. And such abrupt action could only mean trouble.

The public-address system clicked on. "Men, this is the captain speaking. We are proceeding to the scene of a B-52 crash about 300 miles southwest of Guam. We will arrive around midnight to rendezvous with the *Barb* [another nuclear sub] and attempt to find and pick up survivors." There was a pause. "The bomber's crewmen have bailed out squarely in the path of Typhoon Rita. So we'll be rigging for heavy seas and making other special preparations. That is all."

Grumbling ceased. Here at last was real action, and of a welcome kind for an attack sub—a chance to save lives. But elation was tempered with concern, for our craft was neither built nor equipped for this kind of mission.

Nearly as big as a light cruiser, and displacing 5000 tons, the multimillion-dollar *Gurnard* is as sophisticated as a moon-going spaceship. She, like her sister nukes, can hide silently and almost indefinitely in the black ocean depths, or, far below the worst storms, race to any point needed. With her remarkable detection and weapons systems she can hunt down an enemy sub—or a task force—and nail it.

But the same things that give us our shark-like maneuverability underwater make us clumsy on top. The *Gurnard* is as unwieldy as a barge, even in a calm harbor. On the surface, in high waves, her cigar-shaped hull will roll and wallow like a crippled whale.

Moreover, her conning tower or "sail," rising 35 feet (over three stories) above the waterline, can be entered, in a rough sea, only through the small bridge hatch at the top. And worse, her sail-planes (diving-control fins), jutting like aircraft wings from each side of the tower, pose formidable obstructions in trying to pull any survivor aboard.

Finally, we submariners, submerged much of the time (260 of the past 365 days, in this case), seldom get good at such quaint arts as handling lines or working on pitching decks. But there were no other ships within a day's reach of the survivors.

Our skipper, Cmdr. Clyde R. Bell, 41, visited every section of the sub and organized the 140 men into small brainstorming groups. "Work on how to get survivors alongside and aboard without injuring them," he said. "We don't have the equipment, so we'll have to *invent* it."

The *Gurnard* reached the disaster vicinity about 11 p.m.

"Surface, surface, surface!" blared the p.a. system, and our sub lurched up into the storm. Immediately, a great wave crashed on our bow, driving our nose down and sending us into an accidental dive. "Back emergency! Full rise stern planes!" The ship shuddered with this full-speed-in-reverse effort. The helmsman yelled, "Depth 145 feet and we're still going down!" Finally, the sub's impromptu descent was arrested. At an instrument panel in Engine Control, I worked with shaking hands. Faces around me were white. It was not an encouraging beginning.

Some 30 miles away, as the *Barb* surfaced, a series of mountainous waves struck her broadside, sending her into a fast roll. As she listed to the 50-degree point, men found themselves almost standing on the walls, or dangling from supports. Almost on her beam, she caught herself and began to come back upright. Then, swinging about to head into the waves, the *Barb* attained a precarious stability and was ready to begin her search.

From the control center directly beneath the conning tower, Cmdr. John G. Juergens, 39, and four men climbed the high, pitching ladder up to the bridge. They opened the hatch and stepped out into the wild, pitch-black night. The shrieking storm, with gusts up to 100 m.p.h., was heaving up seas so high that every other wave or so swept over their small cockpit. Safety harnesses kept the men from being washed overboard.

Yet two men, Lt. Ron Ricci and Chief Torpedoman Jon Hentz, dared climb out onto the port-side sailplane. Dipping into the angry sea on every port roll, they managed to attach a Jacob's ladder to the sail for bringing aboard survivors.

Overhead, storm-buffeted airplanes from Guam and the Philippines circled, keeping faithful vigil on the downed airmen bobbing on the sea in tiny survival-kit rafts. Twice in the next hour, a low-skimming Navy P-3 Orion got a radar fix on the *Barb* and, with radio and searchlights, directed her toward the nearest raft. As the sub turned, her nose dug in and a wall of water buried the men strapped to her tower. By the time the ship maneuvered, the raft had blown too far away. The *Barb* was directed to a second raft, which swooped up on a wave crest only 40 feet away. A line was shot to the raft but there was no response.

Together, the storm and the darkness were too much. Commander Juergens took his soaked and frustrated topside unit below and ordered the hatch shut. Half of the 130 crewmen—no more accustomed to typhoon seas than a landlubber—were violently seasick.

On the *Gurnard*, too, scores of our men were so sick that, in less demanding circumstances, they would have been in the rack. About 2 or 3 a.m., the decision was reluctantly made to wait until morning, and we slipped back into the quiet depths. But few of us got much sleep. Wide-eyed men sat drinking coffee, hashing over various plans to bring survivors into the ship—and thinking what it must be like up there adrift in that typhoon.

Capt. LeRoy Johnson lay alone in the tiny one-man raft that was part of his survival kit. He had been in the sea for 19 hours—ever since his huge B-52 had inexplicably gone out of control, and he and his crew had had to "punch out!" Now, he could hear the hiss of each comber as it approached. Each time, he braced himself for the swooping, roller-coaster ride, then bailed out the raft when the wave was past. Because he had already capsized several times, he had tied himself in.

The two Air Force officers whom the Barb had so briefly spotted had climbed into one of the dozens of seven-man rafts which an Air Force cargo plane had dropped in the rescue area. The pair were exhausted from the incessant bailing, and from trying to stay upright. They had seen an enormous black cross, eerily lighted and with figures standing on it, rise from the sea and loom for a moment above them before it sank behind a wave—the Barb's conning tower. Could they hold out until the sub rescued them? Then, about 4 or 5 a.m., a third officer paddled his raft over to theirs and joined them.

In a large raft by himself, Airman Dan Johansen had it easier. With his more lightly weighted rubber float buoyantly tobogganing up and down the watery slopes, he was able—remembering his survival training—to relax and try to get some sleep. Now and then he succeeded.

At daylight, we surfaced and resumed the search, following directions from the planes. The Gurnard was rolling so hard that her sailplanes dug into the water on each side. "We're not putting any people up on the bridge until we see something to justify the risk," the captain announced.

Our periscope scanned the ocean. Soon it peered down into a rubber raft, and later into another. Both were empty.

About 8 a.m. we approached a third raft, and the cry came from the conning station, "There's somebody in there!" Then, as the head of the prone, still figure in the raft moved: "He's alive!"

The 40-foot ladder up to *Gurnard*'s bridge was swinging like a pendulum, but Commander Bell made it up, followed by Lt. Cmdr. Ed Morgan, Chief Torpedoman Bill Nielsen and Torpedoman Harold Hermann, the ship's best swimmer, ready in a wet suit. Cracking orders down the bridge telephone, Morgan maneuvered the sub toward the raft, at one moment level with the high bridge on a giant wave; the next, 50 feet below it.

Chief Nielsen put the line-throwing gun to his shoulder and fired. The projectile arced out perfectly, dropping the trailing line right across the little raft and into the hands of Air Force Capt. LeRoy Johnson. He grabbed the line and tugged—but it parted! The sub approached once more, and Nielsen made another flawless shot with the line gun. Again the light nylon strand snapped. As the exhausted pilot tried to sit up in his plunging raft, Commander Bell grabbed the power horn. "Don't waste your strength," he shouted. "We are *not* leaving! We'll be with you until you are safely aboard this ship!"

Wedging himself into a corner of the bridge cockpit, Nielsen feverishly jury-rigged heavier line to the gun's projectile. Meanwhile, Morgan lined the ship up for a third pass.

Down in Engine Control, the engine-change bells were dinging like toyland on Christmas Eve. Near my station, the sweating throttleman was spinning his three-foot wheel almost constantly. Normally he executes about 15 "bell changes" a day. This time it was 150 on that two-hour watch!

But now, as the order "Full astern" came to slow down the ship, a tiny wire in an electric regulator melted, and a sobering report went up from the engine room: "We have lost No. 2 main generator. We can give you only limited power."

Nonetheless, up on the bridge, Commander Morgan managed one more flawless approach. Nielsen shot off his makeshift missile of heavier nylon. Whirling out in crazy spirals through the rain, it settled—and the flier had the line in his hands. This time it didn't break, and the pilot used it to pull a thick tow rope to his raft. Then our men began hauling him toward the sub.

Plan A was to bring him up the forward side of our high conning tower, which was like a wildly swinging, wet, windowless silo. A boarding ladder—two cargo nets lashed together and weighted with heavy steel bars—was to be dangled from the bridge. We assembled all the gear but then realized there was too much equipment to get up to the bridge, and abandoned this plan.

So backup Plan B was immediately ordered. It consisted of a gigantic, clumsy piece of "fishing tackle." The "hook," a homemade sling-type harness, was tossed down to the flier, who struggled into it. The line ran up the "pole" of the sub's hydraulic antenna mast and down the hatch. In a passageway some 50 feet below stood a double file of 15 sailors—the "reel power."

Commander Morgan waited for the strategic moment when the ship would be starting down into a wave trough, the raft starting up on a crest. "Take up the slack," he ordered. Someone pulled a lever and the hydraulic mast started up, first snapping the line taut and then, as it shot to its full height, jerking the pilot from the raft. He dangled in midair, in peril of being bashed against the tower's side.

"Pulling detail . . . *Heave! Heave!*"

Below, the men slipped and scrambled, trying to keep an even strain on the line. As the sub took a hard roll, most of them fell, but all kept pulling until the order came, "Avast heaving! Ease her down!"

Captain Johnson, dangling over the narrow bridge, was lowered into four pairs of reaching hands. "Thanks," he said. And then, staring in semiconscious amazement at the contraption that had helped heave him aboard: "Interesting."

Meanwhile, *Barb* was retrieving other survivors, who, having bailed out of the bomber before their commander, were miles away. Aircraft directed the *Barb* to the three Air Force officers lying exhausted in their single large raft. Getting the nod from Skipper Juergens, lank, steel-muscled Chief Torpedoman Jon Hentz, the *Barb's* best scuba diver, plunged into the mountainous waves to carry a tow line toward the raft 200 feet away.

He risked being killed by the ship, which lurched so high above him he could see the barnacles on its bottom. On the swim, he went under several times. But he made it. The three airmen were fished out one at a time and pulled by sheer muscle power up to the bridge.

The *Barb* was then directed to the raft containing Dan Johansen. Standing on the deck of the sub's lunging sailplane, Electronics Technician Gerry Spaulding fired a direct line-gun hit on the raft. Johansen caught the line on the fly and was soon hauled aboard with a sling.

Long before the *Barb* and *Gurnard* reached Guam, congrat-ulations and awards were pouring in on the ships' radios for our part in the joint Air Force–Navy mercy mission—"one of the most difficult in our history," as Defense Secretary Melvin Laird called it. Each ship got a Meritorious Unit Commenda-tion, and the ten submariners who played perilous topside roles received individual commendations.

As someone said later, back on Guam: "The Navy hasn't changed a bit, in one respect, since the days of John Paul Jones. That typhoon showed us that the most important thing, even on the fanciest super-ships, is still men—seamen."

Beyond the Call of Duty
in Vietnam

BY KENNETH Y. TOMLINSON

Braving heavy communist gunfire one muggy afternoon in April 1969, helicopter pilot Lt. Robert Vinson picked up eight seriously wounded men deep in the treacherous Ashau Valley of Vietnam, and flew them to the base hospital. It was the end of three grueling days of combat and resupply missions for this 23-year-old from Belmont, Massachusetts. In that time, he had seen four of his squadron's helicopters shot down and three pilots killed.

But, weary as he was, Vinson had still another mission he wanted to fly. Right after debriefing, he took a chopper 20 miles north to a village nestled among the rice paddies of the Huongdien Peninsula, just below the Demilitarized Zone. He trudged through a muddy field to a half-finished school. Surveying the work, he said to a Vietnamese builder, "We're going to need more cement. I'll have some here in a few days."

In the last year, even while fighting communism, Vinson has been engaged in a personal war of his own—against sickness and ignorance in rural Vietnam. When he first visited the isolated Huongdien Peninsula in early 1969, three poorly equipped medical dispensaries served 34,000 people. There were only nine schools, each riddled with bullet holes, and the sole, two-room high school had to hold classes in three shifts. "This is intolerable," he said. "These people must be helped."

Wherever he went thereafter, Vinson was on the lookout for surplus material. Flying a colonel to a briefing in Danang one day, he saw a large stack of two-by-fours piled next to the landing pad. "That lumber could help put 50 kids in a school," he told a supply sergeant. The colonel was flown back to camp with lumber crammed in with him. Vinson scrounged bags of rain-damaged cement, tin and lumber from ammunition boxes. Other helicopter crewmen joined in to help, and every effort they made was matched by the people of Huongdien. After Vinson's 158th Aviation Battalion donated $1000 for an addition to the high school, the South Vietnamese district chief searched for funds for a second building.

What has it all meant to Huongdien? Five dispensaries have been constructed and stocked with medical supplies. Six new schools have been built, while the nine others have been repaired. The high school now has eight rooms—and a library. The day before Vinson left Vietnam last January, village and hamlet chiefs honored him in a simple ceremony. The district chief said, "We can never thank you enough."

All over South Vietnam our soldiers are engaged in similar humanitarian missions. An artilleryman from New Jersey spends a free afternoon stacking sandbags at an orphanage outside Pleiku so the children will be protected from communist mortar attacks. An Army engineer from California distributes toys he bought in Hong Kong to the Longbinh orphans his unit adopted. A Marine rifleman from Texas, on his way in from an all-night patrol near Danang, stops to treat huge sores on the back of an old Vietnamese man. The list of individual acts of mercy is unending. In fact, as one senior military officer told me, "My hardest task is keeping track of the incurable humanitarianism of our troops."

Last year U.S. Army volunteers helped construct 1253 schools and 597 hospitals and dispensaries, contributing $300,000 from their own pockets. Personnel of the Third Marine Amphibious Force helped build 268 classrooms, 75 dispensaries and hospitals, and 78 churches, temples and pagodas. The $40,000 contributed by Marines to a scholarship fund ensured an education for 935 children. Air Force men gave personal and financial assistance to 1218 schools, medical facilities and orphanages. Air Force doctors, dentists and medics treated 390,000 Vietnamese in volunteer programs.

One shining example is the 120-bed Hoakhanh children's hospital, dedicated early in 1969, and one of the most modern of its kind in the Far East. Financed with money raised by combat Marines, it is an outgrowth of smaller, crowded hospitals and roadside dispensaries, where Marines and Navy corpsmen had volunteered their help to sick and injured children. There are two operating rooms, isolation facilities and a maternity ward equipped with incubators; 25 Vietnamese nurses are being trained to work in the new facilities. Last year, 16,000 children were treated at the hospital, many of whom would otherwise have died.

As I walked through the main ward earlier this year, I saw a wiry boy of 11 playing games with a group of visiting Marines. Seven months before, he had been caught in a fire and brought in with burns over 75 percent of his body. He told my interpreter: "All my life I will never forget this place and these healing people. Some way I will repay them."

Meet some of the countless other "healing people" involved in helping the South Vietnamese:

The "new parents" of the American Division. When Capt. Charles Adams, a 27-year-old Protestant chaplain from Springfield, Missouri, visited Binhson Catholic Orphanage in Quangngai Province in May 1969, 60 children were subsisting on one or two bowls of rice a day and sleeping on the floors of a school. The chaplain told a group of men in the American Division's Fifth Battalion, 46th Infantry, about the situation, and they eagerly agreed to help. "Don't worry, chaplain," said one veteran sergeant. "Those kids have just got themselves some new parents."

Combat troops began sacking food from captured enemy caches—sometimes as much as 500 pounds a week—and shipping it back on returning helicopters. Mess sergeants at battalion headquarters set aside surplus food. Soldiers found 40 Army cots in a salvage dump, repaired them, and for the first time the orphans slept in beds. On payday, troops in the field passed cups for contributions. Ten percent of poker winnings was earmarked for the Binhson orphans. By the end of the year an eight-room, cinder-block structure had been built to house them.

The battalion's 800 men continue to give $400 a month.

They want the orphanage—just one of the 350 helped by our servicemen—to be self-sufficient by the time our troops leave Vietnam. The first small step toward this goal: 15 pigs and 22 ducks purchased for Binhson.

Servicemen who become friends of outcasts. Air Force pilots visiting a relocated (because of Vietcong harassment) leper colony on the shores of Danang Bay last year were shocked by what they saw. Some 240 lepers and their children were living in primitive huts and tents. Masses of flies swarmed around helpless lepers in a makeshift hospital. "I'm coming back to help these people," said Lt. William Kruger, 25, an Air Force Academy graduate. His companions felt the same way.

Soon there were more weekend volunteers—Air Force, Army and Marines—than could be transported to the isolated beach, which was without a dock. Improvised building materials—lumber, sheet metal—were thrown overboard 50 yards from shore and guided in by GIs standing shoulder-deep in water. By the time monsoon rains began last fall, the men had 40 houses built for the lepers.

Quartermaster First Class Sam Lopiccolo—village builder. Soon after the U.S. Navy moved into the lower Camau Peninsula, a longtime communist stronghold, a group of refugees wanted to settle nearby for protection. Lopiccolo, 27, of Waterloo, New York, salvaged material to help them build a village. In three weeks 500 families had settled along the once-barren banks of the Cualon River.

All this did not go unnoticed by the Vietcong: a dozen villagers were soon kidnapped, while two others were shot when they refused to pay V.C. tax collectors. Booby traps were set around the perimeter of the village, and the Vietcong put a price on Sam Lopiccolo's head. Undiscouraged, he and the villagers began constructing a school. After guerrillas slipped into the village early one morning and blew up the partially completed structure, Lopiccolo and the people doggedly rebuilt it.

Sam Lopiccolo now is helping the people of a newer village downstream build a school for their children. He has twice extended his tours of duty in Vietnam and is now in his third year. "This job can't be done in one year or two," he explains. "That's why I stay."

Chief Warrant Officer George Railey—orphanage counselor. Working night after night while finishing his third tour in Vietnam, this Special Forces veteran built a merry-go-round for the children of an orphanage near Pleiku. (The carrousel turns on the discarded axle of a 2 1/2-ton truck. The horses are made from salvage metal. Its centerpiece is a gaily painted gasoline tank.) During the dry season the orphanage's sole source of water was a 1200-gallon tank truck Railey drove. He used a chain saw to cut firewood for cooking during his lunch hour. Each day he picked up three teenage orphans and took them to his shop, where he and his men trained them to be mechanics.

Railey methodically visited eight remote Montagnard villages twice each month, distributing gifts and surplus food to the often-hungry hill tribesmen of the Central Highlands. When I traveled to these villages with Railey last January, he was awaiting confirmation of a fourth year's extension of duty in Vietnam. He told me he had found new meaning in life, working with the suffering victims of war. That work tragically ended three months later. He was killed in an accident while taking presents to Montagnard refugees at Letrung.

Sgt. Richard Pellerin—medic to the Montagnards. Pellerin, 27, who joined the Army after dropping out of the University of Michigan Medical School, is one of two medics who alternate duties at Pleidjereng, one of many Special Forces camps located at strategic hot spots along the Cambodian border. One medic is always out on patrol. The other operates the camp dispensary and goes down to the primitive Montagnard village of Pleidoch three times a week to help the sick.

I watched Pellerin treat a young woman, badly burned when she had rolled into a fire a few nights before; her leprosy-deadened senses had not alerted her to the pain. A small boy waited to lead us to his sick father. Seeing the child lifted the spirit of the intense young medic. "When I got here, nearly every kid in this village had trachoma, an eye infection," Pellerin said. "Now we would have to go looking for a case to treat."

Sgt. First Class Lonnie Johnson—jack-of-all-help. When the 36-year-old Green Beret learned that a mother in the remote mountain village of Dongbathin was having difficulty in childbirth, he made his way to her home, carried her to a truck and raced to Camranh, where a Navy doctor successfully delivered the baby. After a Vietcong rocket killed eight Nhatrang civilians last September, Johnson found tin and wood to build the survivors a new home. Last Christmas he gave 1500 orphans toothpaste, soap, candy and nuts collected from fellow servicemen.

As Johnson and I sat on our bunks at a Special Forces camp at Pleiku, I asked him why he has done so much for the Vietnamese. "I was raised by my grandparents, who were sharecroppers on a farm in Alabama," he said. "We were very poor. I got one pair of overalls to last a year. My shirts were made from fertilizer sacks. When I got to Vietnam and saw these people and their children, I remembered what it was like. I made up my mind I was going to do everything I could for them."

Everywhere I traveled in Vietnam, I saw men like these. Yet their amazing humanitarian accomplishments are nearly always overlooked amid daily battle reports and domestic conflict over the war itself.

"The number of our GIs who devote their free time, energy and money to aid the Vietnamese would surprise you," declared Bob Hope at the end of his latest Christmas tour of U.S. bases there. "But maybe it wouldn't," he added. "I guess you know what kind of guys your sons and brothers and the kids next door are."

★ ★ ★

A Hero Comes Home

BY KENNETH O. GILMORE

This is a story of one brave soldier who has come home from Vietnam. His name: Christopher J. O'Sullivan. He was born and brought up in the outskirts of New York City but he could have been from anywhere across our land.

Chris was ten when the family moved to a third-floor walk-up in Astoria near LaGuardia Airport, in 1946. "We'll be living above a candy store," his father, William O'Sullivan, announced grandly to Chris and his three-year-old sister, Hanora. Actually, it was a soda fountain and newsstand, but everyone called it the "candy store."

The family's piano was hoisted up outside the building, and into the small front parlor. Bill O'Sullivan and his wife Anna both loved music, and over the years they had many a session around the piano, the whole family singing. In Ireland, Bill had learned a hundred ditties, including "An Irish Soldier Boy" with its woeful words: *"Goodby, God bless you, Mother dear, I hope your heart won't pain, but pray to God your soldier boy, your son, you'll see again."*

Chris loved the lore of Ireland, but what fascinated him most was a snapshot in the family album of a 12-year-old boy standing, rifle in hand. It was Bill O'Sullivan, who during the First World War ran away from home to join the Royal Munster Fusiliers.

"I was big for my age," Bill explained. "I wore my father's pants."

"Gee, that must have been something," Chris said.

"What *was* something, lad," his father replied, "was coming to America when I was just 14."

He meant it. Bill had an unblushing love affair with the U.S.A. "What a fantastic heritage this country has given us," he said. "What a responsibility to live up to it."

In the New York Police Department, Bill O'Sullivan worked up from rookie to detective. He helped a young prosecutor named Thomas Dewey convict some of the nation's worst racketeers. But more than anything he yearned to *show* a son that "heritage" he spoke about. With World War II over and no more gas rationing, he grabbed every free moment for "our weekend rides"—to Albany, to Gettysburg's battlefields, to Valley Forge, and time and again to Williamsburg, the restored capital of the Virginia colony. "This is the most valuable investment we can make," Bill told Anna.

That investment earned one of its countless dividends the winter night when Chris emerged from his room and recited some verses he had written: *"Long years ago our forefathers fought. Let not their gallant battles go for naught. They left a heritage, a land that was free. Remember and preserve that liberty."*

Chris went to Xavier High, a military school run by the Jesuits. There, between athletics and lifting bar bells at night, he grew into lean muscular manhood. At graduation in 1954 he earned not only a silver medal for class excellence but also the American Legion award for the best essay on Americanism.

"Why is it," he wrote, *"that some citizens do not seem to realize that one of the greatest goals in life is the fight for the safety of our democracy and free way of life?"*

He believed it so deeply that he passed up a four-year scholarship elsewhere to enroll at Fordham University; its ROTC program offered him an opportunity to become a U.S. Army officer. After graduation he went through a grueling special-service course to become an airborne ranger—Bill O'Sullivan eagerly read the reports his son sent back from Fort Benning, Georgia. Then it was off to Hawaii for Chris, where he was commissioned a second lieutenant. There too he was joined by a bride, petite blue-eyed Eleanor Scott, who had grown up three blocks from the candy store.

En route back to Fort Dix, New Jersey, after six months' service in Thailand, Chris in 1962 took a 30-day observation tour in Vietnam. He was staggered by the communist terrorism he saw and kept insisting that he be allowed to go back. Finally he got his way. Now the father of two boys—Michael, three, and Stevie, two—Chris drew Bill aside at the airport when he left for Vietnam in September 1964. "Please take over for me," he said. "The boys need a father, and I may be away a long time. And if you can, take them for those weekend rides."

And so, as before, but now with Eleanor and the grandchildren, Bill and Anna went to the places Chris had loved. Meanwhile, above the candy store, Anna O'Sullivan's ear became keenly attuned for the rattle of the front door whenever the postman dropped a letter into the box.

> *Dearest Mom and Dad: . . . Snipers fire a thousand and one shots a day. At night the Vietcong control Vietnam, and soldiers and advisers alike pray for the dawn.*
>
> *Yesterday a mortar round landed ten feet from my jeep. Bullets, mortars, mines, booby-traps and strafing planes are all as accepted as the sound of the BMT subway. I am an adviser to the Vietnamese 39th Ranger Battalion. We are now encamped in a small village. If you have a map . . .*

They already had bought the map, a large one, just to keep track. Bill would spread it out on the dining-room table and try to imagine what was happening at a pinpoint called Duc Pho.

If Eleanor had received a letter, she would bring it when she came every day with the boys, to visit.

> *Dearest Eleanor: This morning a mother approached us carrying a scalded baby. But the Vietcong had controlled this village so long that their tales of American advisers eating children were totally believed. The mother screamed and ran away from me. . . .*

On the newspaper rack outside the candy store, headlines told of a worsening war—the bloody ambushes; the wholesale slaughter of the South Vietnamese; the mounting toll of Americans slain; Washington's painful efforts for a negotiated peace. Late in November an airmail envelope came to Bill O'Sullivan at work. It contained an insurance policy and a message which tightened his stomach:

> *I'm sending this additional insurance coverage to you because I don't want either Eleanor or Mother to know unless the need arises. The Vietcong now outnumber as well as outgun us. We are surrounded here. The Vietcong ambushed me once, killing my driver. I sleep in uniform and socks.*

At the candy store, neighbors asked Bill O'Sullivan about Chris. "He's doing just fine." His voice rang with pride. But whenever the postman rattled the front door, his heartbeat quickened. Once a tape came. Bill put the recording machine on the dining-room table. They listened to a familiar deep voice while jungle birds squawked in the background.

Bill O'Sullivan tried to make it a merry Christmas. He and the boys decorated a tree at the apartment. And in Vietnam Captain O'Sullivan with an armed escort drove 20 miles from Duc Pho to attend Mass and to post a letter.

> *My dear Sons: Tonight is Christmas Eve, and the lonesomeness may be eased if I talk to you. Through your short lives you have brought your mother and me wonderful moments of love and happiness, moments not measured in hours but in heartbeats. I cannot protect you from all the hurts of the world, but I can try to protect you from one of its major dangers. And that is why tonight we are thousands of miles apart.*

Bill O'Sullivan suffered a heart attack in January. "I don't want Chris to be told," he said. "He has enough on his mind." At Columbus Hospital, Anna tried to control her voice as she read to her husband:

> Over here a good fighting unit is used until its soldiers become battle-weary and exhausted. It is a tragedy that has only one ending. This battalion will someday be bled dry.

Bled dry . . . Bill's hand reached out and met Anna's. In March Chris wrote to Eleanor:

> Here away from the phony atmosphere of the hotel heroes there is little sham. I've been afraid many times, but I can think, advise and command in spite of it. But I now have fear as a constant companion. As my time with the battalion is closing, I'm afraid of being afraid. There's an axiom here that the first and last months are the most dangerous for a field adviser.

April was the month that Chris was supposed to end his six months' combat duty and take a desk job. But his Vietnamese counterpart asked him to remain. *As you trained me, Dad, there was only one decision. My duty was to remain.* So Chris stayed on. He had a fungus infection on his hands, intestinal disorders and dysentery. His blond hair had turned gray, and he'd dropped from 186 to 156 pounds.

On Easter weekend in Washington at a gigantic "Get Out of Vietnam" rally, one speaker compared a Vietcong terrorist with

Jesus Christ. And the crowd cheered. "It's a strange thing," Bill O'Sullivan told Anna. "Isn't there any cheering for our soldiers who are helping hold off the communists?"

Two days later, on April 19, a ferocious Vietcong force struck the 39th Battalion. For two hours, under murderous fire, Captain O'Sullivan darted from one gun position to another to direct a counter-barrage. He hit 15 Vietcong and saved 75 of his own men trapped by the enemy. His six-foot-two frame was so often out in the open that shouts of "Shoot the American!" could be heard above the roar of battle. From that day on, the Vietcong put up a $500 reward for O'Sullivan's head.

In America, at college and university campuses across the land, the fad for denouncing the war in Vietnam mounted. Was the war merely a maneuver to reach a meaningless settlement? Bill O'Sullivan studied again an oft-read special letter:

> *I firmly believe in the fight. No solution is so damning as to allow the communists to seize more men, women and children here. Those Vietnamese who care don't want a neutral slavery. They want the free choice of their future. And this can occur only if you and I see a purpose for the fighting—to help these people live and grow free.*
>
> *This country, like our own in 1776, must receive help.*

As May 1965 drew to a close, Captain O'Sullivan at last was ordered to Saigon and rest. On his way he checked into Quang Ngai. But on Saturday the 29th, a hundred Vietnamese and three Americans were trapped by the Vietcong in a nearby hamlet. All were believed lost. One was Lt. Donald Robison, who had served with Chris virtually the entire time he had been in Vietnam.

Sick with worry, Chris waited at the small Quang Ngai airport for word on Robison. Late that night he wrote a letter to Eleanor, and next morning he led a ranger counterattack. Suddenly his 300-man force was in grave trouble. More than 800 Vietcong sprang from hidden jungle tunnels. In a field of death, Chris helped carry off the wounded and, by radio, directed air strikes. He warned that ammunition was running dangerously low.

Then it happened.

Charging up a hill with Sgt. Willie D. Tyrone, he was hit by shrapnel. The sergeant carried him to the hilltop and radioed back news of his death. When helicopter relief arrived, they also found Tyrone's riddled body. Around them lay more than a hundred South Vietnamese rangers, all disemboweled. They had fought to the last man.

It was Memorial Day in America. Bill and Anna had taken Eleanor and the children to the Catskills. On Monday they returned to Astoria and dropped Eleanor and the boys off at their home. Only minutes later Eleanor was at the candy store running up the stairs clutching the telegram. Her red eyes told the old detective: his son was gone.

Tuesday morning the tragedy was a squib in the New York papers. At Eleanor's home the phone rang with condolences. One voice, however, was unfamiliar:

"Is this Mrs. O'Sullivan? I'd just like to say how *glad* I am your husband is dead. He got what he deserved. He shouldn't have been in Vietnam. He should have died in a worse way." A sharp *click.*

Eleanor O'Sullivan stared at the phone, then crumpled to the floor, unconscious.

Next morning the phone carried another gloating taunt. "It was a good thing he was killed," a different voice told Eleanor.

On Wednesday afternoon Maj. Reginald Grier, who had served with Chris in Hawaii, came by. Once more the phone rang, and Major Grier grabbed at the receiver.

"I just called to tell Mrs. O'Sullivan how *happy* I am that her husband was killed in Vietnam." It was a man's voice, well modulated, controlled, almost as if the caller were reading professionally from a script. "I want you to know this: the communists will eventually win in Vietnam." Then he hung up.*

Thursday morning a final letter arrived in Chris's handwriting:

> *Dearest Eleanor: Tonight my heart is sadder than it has ever been. Tomorrow we are going to look for Don and his two sergeants. I can only ask your forgiveness because in this operation I am going to do all that is necessary to find Don or his body.*

---

*In at least five other cases, the wives and relatives of soldiers killed in Vietnam have reported similar calls —apparently not crank calls but ideologically motivated harassment. The family of one dead soldier got a postcard demanding that his insurance money be donated to the Vietcong.

I promised you I would be overly cautious now that I am "rotating" so soon. I cannot keep that promise. Don has a young wife and a three-year-old daughter. If he was looking for me, you would want him to do the best job he could. By the time you receive this letter, it will be all over one way or another. Tonight I pray it will be for the best. God have mercy on both of us. Love, Chris.

June 9 dawned clear in New York. Christopher O'Sullivan had come home . . . to be buried. An Army honor guard formed a corridor as the flag-draped coffin was carried 50 feet along Ditmars Boulevard, through the overflow crowd, from funeral home to the packed Immaculate Conception Church for solemn requiem Mass. Prowl cars cruised a two-block area, and riot vans parked nearby. New York Police Commissioner Vincent Broderick personally commanded a 30-man security force on the scene. For it was feared the services might be turned into a demonstration against the U.S. role in Vietnam.

At sunset August 11 on a parade ground at Governors Island, across from Manhattan, Eleanor O'Sullivan, her children by her side, stepped forward. In behalf of her husband she accepted six medals, including the Distinguished Service Cross for "extraordinary heroism" last April 19, the Silver Star for "gallantry in action" on May 30, the Purple Heart for his mortal wounds. Bill and Anna stood by.

A cannon boomed. The clear notes of taps echoed across the field. As the First Army Band played "The Star-Spangled Banner," Stevie and Michael saluted with the soldiers. And Bill could almost hear Chris speaking the words he had written in a recent letter:

> *Here is a country—Vietnam—with people like you and me, with families like ours, fighting for the right to determine its existence. As long as you and I believe we should be free, we must treat that feeling in others as important. So if God wills I die here, there is no finer cause today for which a man must die than the cause of these people.*

THE BOSNIAN WAR

★ ★ ★

Pilot Down:
The Rescue of Scott O'Grady

BY MALCOLM McCONNELL

Air Force Capt. Scott O'Grady eased his F-16C fighter close beside the one piloted by his flight leader, Capt. Bob Wright. Through breaks in the clouds, they saw the green mountains of Bosnia far below. Their mission that afternoon of June 2, 1995, was a routine combat air patrol policing a NATO "No Fly Zone." For months no Bosnian Serb plane had challenged NATO fighters in this sector, and intelligence had reported the zone free of surface-to-air missiles (SAMs).

Suddenly O'Grady and Wright were jarred by the buzz and amber flash of their cockpit missile-warning instruments. "Missile in the air!" Wright called urgently.

Two supersonic SA-6 SAMs, hidden by the overcast, were streaking toward the F-16s. Seconds later the missiles ripped through the clouds, exhaust plumes trailing. Wright and O'Grady threw their aircraft into evasive maneuvers. One missile slashed harmlessly past Wright's plane. The other scored a direct hit on the belly of O'Grady's fighter. Horrified, Wright watched the wings crumple and an orange fireball blossom around the cockpit. Then O'Grady's jet, canopy intact, disappeared into the clouds.

"Basher 52 took a direct hit—he's down," Wright radioed.

"Any parachute?"

"Negative."

Flames seared O'Grady's neck and licked under his helmet visor, singeing his eyebrows, as his F-16 tore through the cloud bank. The 29-year-old pilot could smell his hair burning. *Eject!* O'Grady's left hand groped for the yellow ejection-seat handle between his knees. *Let it work,* he prayed.

The jet's Plexiglas canopy detached, and the seat's rocket charge fired. Seconds later, O'Grady heard the reassuring twang of his opening chute. He felt his heart pounding as he floated into clear sky. *I can't believe I'm alive.* Hanging beneath him on a tether, his survival pack whipped in the wind.

O'Grady was relieved to see that the winds were pushing him toward a brushy field and away from the orange-tiled roofs of the town of Bosanski Petrovac, a Bosnian Serb stronghold. He noticed hills rising to a green plateau about two miles to the southeast.

Then his stomach wrenched as he saw men in uniform pointing at him from a military truck parked along a highway. When he hit a clearing near the road, O'Grady jumped up, unsnapped his parachute and shucked off his helmet. He needed a hiding place *now*.

Snatching his survival pack, O'Grady stumbled through the brush and, like a rabbit, burrowed into thick foliage, forcing himself deeper with his knees and elbows until he was completely covered.

He heard men calling to each other. *They know I'm here.* On his stomach, face thrust into the dirt, O'Grady tried to conceal his neck and ears with his green flight gloves. He heard boots thumping close by. O'Grady lay absolutely still, breathing shallowly. *At least they don't have dogs*, he thought. *At least Wright saw me eject.*

More than five thousand miles away in Skokie, Illinois, Stacy O'Grady stood on a ladder, helping decorate the gym of the school where she taught eighth grade. "Ms. O'Grady," a student interrupted, "your mother's on the phone."

Why would Mom call from Seattle? she wondered. *Scott!* Stacy scrambled down the ladder and raced to the teacher's lounge. Her mother confirmed her fears: Scott's plane had been hit by a missile; no one knew where Stacy's brother was, and no further contact had been made since the incident.

Stacy left school immediately and packed a bag to join her father, Dr. Bill O'Grady, a radiologist, at his home in Alexandria, Virginia. All she could think of was the time she and her mother had proudly pinned gold lieutenant bars on Scott. He had been so happy that day. It capped a youth devoted to adventure: sky diving, gliding, bobsledding. Stacy couldn't believe that Scott had not survived.

Aboard the amphibious-helicopter ship USS *Kearsarge*, 20 miles off the Balkan coast in the northern Adriatic, Col. Martin Berndt assembled members of the 24th Marine Expeditionary Unit, who were specially trained in combat search and rescue. Intelligence reports now confirmed that the ambush of the two F-16s had been a clever deception. The Bosnian Serbs knew that if the SA-6 mobile missiles had tried to track O'Grady and Wright directly, the cockpit instruments in the F-16s would have detected the radar immediately.

Instead, they had relied on civilian radars across the border in the Serb Republic. The data were processed at an air-defense center in Belgrade, then transmitted by landline to three mobile SA-6 missile vehicles in the mountains near Bihac. Only at the last instant did SA-6 operators launch the missiles and then turn on their radar—giving the young pilots virtually no warning.

Berndt tapped the large tactical wall map of northern Bosnia. Normally helicopter rescues were conducted under cover of darkness, with the pilots wearing night-vision goggles. But goggles couldn't detect power lines that snaked across the valleys. To avoid the SAMs, the rescue team might have to risk flying in daylight, threading their way along valleys, but that would expose them to anti-aircraft guns and shoulder-fired missiles.

Berndt looked at Maj. Bill Tarbutton, 43, who would command the rescue aircraft, and Lt. Col. Chris Gunther, also 43, who would lead the rescue team on the ground. "Right now," he told them, "the big questions are: Is O'Grady alive, and if so, where is he?"

Rifle fire cracked near O'Grady's hiding place, and bullets whipped through nearby brush. Instinctively, he thrust his face deeper into the dirt. They were shooting to kill. O'Grady prayed, trying to focus all of his concentration on the familiar words *Our Father, who art in heaven* . . .

Out of the corner of his eye, O'Grady could see shadows six feet away. Weapons rattled against branches as the soldiers made their way through the brush, using their rifle muzzles as probes. The men with the guns seemed to be circling him, toying with him. *Holy Mary, Mother of God, pray for us sinners* . . . Soon the voices faded, and the rifles cracked from farther away.

Finally the sun passed below the western mountains. O'Grady heard the irritating, high-pitched whine of gnats and mosquitoes as they hovered about him. But he forced himself to continue lying motionless, his mouth dry from terror and thirst. When darkness fell, he could risk moving. He was determined to reach that plateau away from the highway and the town—the best place for pickup by a rescue helicopter.

For two days the Marines aboard the *Kearsarge* had been on one-hour alert—but there was still no word on O'Grady's fate. Bosnian Serb TV had shown the wreckage of O'Grady's plane and announced that he had been captured. Major Tarbutton was skeptical. "If the Serbs had O'Grady," he said, "they'd show him on TV."

Colonel Berndt agreed. Later, an intelligence intercept reached him: Bosnian Serb soldiers had found a parachute, but not the pilot.

O'Grady estimated that he had covered less than a mile in three nights. But he'd worked by the book, moving only at night and finding secure hiding places well before dawn.

He thought about his survival equipment. In his vest, the evasion map, radio, and smoke and signal flares were vital, and so was the Global Positioning System (GPS) receiver. This palm-size set processed signals from navigation satellites, giving him an accurate ground position and providing exact coordinates for rescue forces.

A separate survival pack contained a spare radio and batteries, a first-aid kit and more flares. He also had a green foil thermal blanket, camouflage netting, face paint to help conceal him, and plastic bags and a sponge to catch and store rain for drinking water.

So far, hunger hadn't been a problem—but thirst was. That afternoon O'Grady had drunk the last of his eight four-ounce pouches of water. His evasion map showed the nearest stream was on the other side of Bosanski Petrovac, in the other direction from where he was headed.

Now, as dawn approached, O'Grady found another secure hiding place, spread his map as a ground sheet, pulled his thermal blanket across his shoulders and draped a camouflage net over his body. He then turned on his survival radio and sent a brief coded signal. As sunrise filled the valley, he tried to get some sleep. *They're not going to capture me*, he vowed.

Television sets in Bill O'Grady's home were left on around the clock. Sitting on a living-room couch, Stacy O'Grady slipped into a shell of emotional numbness, mindlessly clicking the television remote, flipping through the channels, searching in vain for any sign of hope.

Stacy, Scott and their younger brother Paul had grown up in Spokane, Washington. From childhood experiences, Stacy knew that beneath his easy smile and soft-spoken charm, Scott had a tough core.

Stacy chuckled involuntarily, remembering the day when she was in sixth grade and a bully on the school bus was twisting her coat collar, choking her. Scott was smaller and lighter, but he seized the larger kid with a ferocious grip and glared so fiercely that the bully fled in panic.

Stacy was three years younger, but she and Scott shared the same birthday in October; they had always been close. She could picture the delicate silver crucifix she had given Scott before he left to fly fighters overseas. The thought that he was wearing it gave her comfort as she nodded off to sleep.

It was the afternoon of June 6, four days into his ordeal. Half dozing, O'Grady felt the snout of a cow nuzzling between his boots. After the animal left, O'Grady snatched a handful of grass to gnaw. *If cows can live on it, so can I.* But by now his mouth was almost swollen shut from thirst, and he could swallow only a few blades. His eyes hurt, and his skin was badly wrinkled. He knew his dehydration was severe.

Later that night thunder cracked, followed by a downpour. He opened two plastic bags to catch the water. He also took the sponge from his survival kit to soak up the water pooling in his plastic survival pack. O'Grady drank greedily.

After the rain, the night grew colder. He shivered, his soaked flight suit a chilling weight on his body. When it started raining again, he packed his survival equipment. Since there was not much chance anyone would be out on a night like this, he'd risk moving faster toward the high ground.

O'Grady reached the plateau before dawn. A stone fence separated the pastures of the valley from the scrub brush to the south. He found a secure holding point, then set out to locate a landing zone for a rescue helicopter. The only open spot nearby was rocky, narrow and sloping, with a crude fence blocking the far end. He read the display of his GPS set and noted his position on the map.

O'Grady hid again when daylight came but managed to sleep only fitfully. Hunger was nagging him. He noticed brown ants moving through the weeds near his elbow. He tried to scoop a handful, but snagged only a few. They crunched in his mouth with a lemony tang—not much nourishment, but they moistened his tongue.

After sunset, his thirst returned with a vengeance. O'Grady had finished the rainwater, so he pulled off his wet boots and squeezed a few drops of water from his wool socks into a plastic bag. It was rancid, but drinkable. He dozed off in the hours of early darkness.

He was awakened after midnight on June 8 by the blast of heavy anti-aircraft firing nearby. O'Grady took a compass bearing on the sound. Seconds later he heard a low-flying jet. It had to be a NATO reconnaissance plane looking for him. O'Grady stood cautiously, switched his survival radio to beeper, and pressed the transmit button. *This'll light up the world*, he mused. Both the NATO search planes and the Bosnian Serbs would hear the transmission. He had to wait to see who would find him first.

Just after 1:30 a.m. on June 8, Capt. T. O. Hanford and his wingman, Capt. Vaughn Litdejohn, were flying high above the dark mountains. After a report of a "possible beeper," Hanford was trying to contact O'Grady. For the next 40 minutes he called on the rescue channel. But there was no reply. At 2:07 a.m., with fuel low, Hanford tried O'Grady one last time. "Basher 52, this is Basher 11."

O'Grady's heart raced as he heard Hanford's voice. "Basher 11," he called. "Help!"

Hanford had to verify that the weak voice was O'Grady's. "Basher 52, what was your squadron in Korea?" Hanford asked.

"Juvats," O'Grady replied.

"Copy that," Hanford said, trying to keep his emotions in check. "You're alive. Good to hear your voice." For the next ten minutes Hanford circled as O'Grady used a voice code to reveal his GPS coordinates. Then Hanford told O'Grady he'd be picked up "mañana."

"No," O'Grady replied. "I have to get out tonight."

Hanford reported back to his controllers, then to O'Grady. "You will be rescued, but you have to be prepared to signal in visual range." He added: "If you have an emergency, Basher 52, I will always be monitoring this channel."

In Virginia, the phone rang at 12:48 a.m. "Another reporter," Bill O'Grady said, groaning, as he pulled himself awake. It was Scott's wing commander, Col. Charles F. Wald. "Dr. O'Grady, we've contacted him," Wald said. "He's alive. And we're going to go get him."

Overcome with emotion, the doctor raced to tell Stacy and Paul.

In the pastel dawn, the flight deck of the *Kearsarge* throbbed with the beat of the big helicopters' rotors. From a cockpit jump seat in Dash Two, one of two Super Stallion helicopters, Berndt's headphones crackled. "Pulling power," he heard Tarbutton call from the lead helicopter, Dash One, and then Berndt watched it rise.

There were now four choppers in a trail formation: Dash One and Dash Two, and two smaller Cobra gunships to guard the flanks. Far above them were two Harrier jets, launched from the *Kearsarge*. Across the northern Adriatic, NATO warplanes were assembling a protective umbrella for the Marine rescue effort. At 5:43 a.m., they received the command to cross the Balkan coast.

They flew fast and low—no higher than 500 feet—to evade radar. Ahead, the mountains rose in a dark wall, silhouetted by the sunrise. In Dash One, Tarbutton saw that the valleys were choked with ground fog. This would shield them from visual detection, but make navigating tricky.

"Twenty," announced an unseen airborne controller, codenamed Magic, in a radar plane far above. They were 20 miles from O'Grady.

"Ten," Magic called. Now Tarbutton ordered the Cobras to press ahead, positively identify O'Grady and check the landing zone.

Marine Maj. Scott Mykleby, lead Cobra pilot, flew his gunship toward the coordinates of O'Grady's position.

"I can see you," O'Grady radioed.

"Talk me on to you, Basher," Mykleby replied. A moment later, he heard O'Grady's excited shout. "You're overhead!"

"Pop smoke," Mykleby directed.

O'Grady pulled the tab on an orange smoke flare. Slowing to a hover, Mykleby searched the slope for the clearing that O'Grady said was nearby. O'Grady's little smoke flare was almost lost in the fog. Then Mykleby threw out a yellow smoke grenade to better mark O'Grady's position.

O'Grady warned Mykleby of the heavy firing he had heard the night before, then pulled on the bright orange knit cap from his survival kit. "I'm wearing an orange hat," he told Mykleby.

"Buster," Mykleby radioed Tarbutton—code for proceed ahead at maximum speed.

Tarbutton throttled up his engines and pulled the control stick into a hard climb. The two Super Stallions slashed across the fog bank and climbed the steep ridge.

The clearing was just large enough for the two Super Stallions to land with minimum clearance between the rotor tips. Marines piled out to form a security perimeter as Mykleby radioed O'Grady: "Run to the helicopter." O'Grady pounded through the thicket, his boots slipping on the wet rocks.

Berndt saw movement in the fog to the left. O'Grady's orange hat was bright in the mist. Sgt. Scott Pfister, crew chief on Dash Two, jumped from the hatch. O'Grady was wobbling, obviously exhausted. "Over here, sir," Pfister shouted. Throwing his arm under the young pilot's shoulder, he pushed O'Grady inside.

A Marine wrapped the pilot in a thermal blanket. O'Grady's hands were cold, wrinkled claws, his bearded face waxy. "Thank you, thank you," he kept saying.

Tarbutton ordered the formation to move up and out at maximum speed, flying only 50 feet above the rolling hillsides, so fast that obstacles rushed by in a blur. They were coming up to the final mountain range when the cockpit warning instruments gave a sharp beep.

Tarbutton caught a glimpse of movement to his left and heard Mykleby's warning: "SAMs in the air!"

Mykleby saw a chalk-white smoke trail corkscrew toward the helicopters from the left. As another missile sailed toward them, Mykleby popped a string of glaring magnesium flares to decoy the shoulder-fired SA-7s' infrared homing warheads. But even as he countered the missiles fired from the left, glowing orange baseballs sailed toward the helicopters from the right, incandescent red tracers of an automatic anti-aircraft gun on the ground. The pilots threw their aircraft into violent zigzags. Sgt. Scott Pfister returned fire with a short, rattling burst from his .50-caliber machine gun.

As O'Grady hunched beneath a blanket, warmth slowly seeping into his chilled limbs, an assault-rifle bullet pierced the Super Stallion's tail ramp and ricocheted wildly around the troop bay. Two feet from O'Grady, Sgt. Major Angel Castro felt a blow on his side. He pulled out the empty canteen from his hip pouch. The green plastic was deeply gouged from the impact of the bullet.

The Cobra pilots wanted to engage the anti-aircraft gun— but if Tarbutton broke the gunships from formation, he'd have no protection crossing the coastal towns ahead. They had to hold course and take fire.

An amber warning light flashed, signaling one of Tarbutton's main rotor blades had been hit. Then Mykleby radioed that he also had a warning light.

Moments later, they flashed across the coastline, and the *Kearsarge* task force came into view on the horizon. "Mother in sight," Tarbutton informed the team.

O'Grady blinked at the dazzling surface of the Adriatic Sea, his face twisted with emotion. Colonel Berndt looked back from the jump seat, and O'Grady flashed a warm grin.

Just after 1:30 a.m. in Alexandria, Bill O'Grady received another call from Colonel Wald. "Scott is aboard the *Kearsarge*," Wald said. "He's dehydrated, but otherwise fine." Scott's father rushed to tell Stacy and Paul the news. The family rejoiced. Stacy began counting down the hours when she would see her brother again.

On June 10, Scott O'Grady addressed reporters at Aviano Air Base in Italy. "If it wasn't for God's love for me," he said, "and my love for God, I wouldn't have gotten through it." But he also reserved special thanks for the "people at the pointy end of the spear"—the Marines who had risked their lives to save him. "If you want to find heroes," he said, "that's where you should look."

THE GULF WAR

★ ★ ★

They Went to War

BY MALCOLM McCONNELL

On a rainy spring night in 1944, a lanky American volunteer attached to the British 8th Army led a platoon of ambulances across the Rapido River in southern Italy. Lewis Harned, just 19 years old, was already a veteran of savage fighting near Monte Cassino, and now Harned was again in desperate straits.

The Allied bridgehead was under German counterattack. His duty was to evacuate the wounded. Suddenly, small-arms fire ripped through nearby trees. "Back!" Harned shouted, throwing his ambulance into reverse. "Germans!"

Later, Harned sat drinking a canteen cup of coffee, still twanging from the spent adrenalin of the encounter. *If I ever get home, he mused, at least I'll know I've been to war.*

Forty-six years later, Lewis Harned, M.D., ran a sports-medicine clinic in Madison, Wisconsin. He and his wife, Sally, married 42 years, had raised five children. But in 1985, he had joined the Wisconsin National Guard, and now, at age 66, he was a full colonel commanding the 13th Evacuation Hospital, an ultra-modern, 400-bed facility that could be transported anywhere.

After the Iraqi invasion of Kuwait in August 1990, Dr. Harned guessed his unit would be activated. On November 15, his phone rang.

"Colonel," his commander said, "put on your uniform. I'll meet you at the armory with all the details."

The scene was typically American: a circle of children on a shady suburban sidewalk encouraging a boy riding a shiny new unicycle. The five O'Connor children grew up on the streets of Godfrey, Illinois, a quiet commuter town across the river from St. Louis. Paula, the middle child, was 12, blond, freckled, a tomboy in blue jeans, always competing with her older brother, Tony.

When their friend had trouble mastering his unicycle, Tony managed half a block before falling.

"Let me try," Paula shouted. She pedaled a whole block before dismounting. Not to be outdone, Tony managed two blocks. Then Paula pumped all the way to St. Ambrose School, a mile away. That night around the dinner table, Joe O'Connor grinned as his daughter described her adventure.

After graduating from high school in 1985, Paula O'Connor enlisted as a mechanic in the Air Force. She had studied auto mechanics and was good with machines.

Joe and Sarah O'Connor were shocked. "Paula," her father, a Korean War veteran, said, "you don't know what you're getting into."

"It's too late," she countered. "I've already signed up."

At Lowry Air Force Base outside Denver, O'Connor—the only woman in her group of 20—learned the demanding skills of a weapons loader, arming F-16 attack jets. Modern missiles and laser-guided bombs have to be assembled and fused with exacting precision, and speed is vital. If O'Connor missed a step, the bomb might miss its target or fail to detonate.

O'Connor spent the next two years assigned to an F-16 NATO tactical fighter wing in Spain. She had proved herself to be one of the best weapons loaders in the unit, yet people still dismissed her as a woman. "I don't know why you're working so hard," one young airman told her. "If there's ever a war, you won't get to go anyway."

In June 1990, Senior Airman Paula O'Connor won a coveted assignment to the 37th Tactical Fighter Wing in Nevada, home of the F-117A Stealth fighter. The unit had been highly classified; all O'Connor knew was that the Stealth was a weird-looking plane that was supposedly invisible to enemy radar. The first day at the base, she stood in wonder beside the big black fighter's strangely angled plates and wedges.

The Stealths navigation and laser-weapons guidance systems made it the most accurate bomber in the world. Because externally hung bombs would be visible on radar, the F-117A carried its munitions in a bay in its belly. This meant the loading crew had to work in tight quarters where a dropped tool, or even an elbow, could damage sensors or delicate guidance systems. O'Connor quickly mastered these skills under the pressure of simulated combat.

In August 1990, the preparations took on urgency. Her unit

was ordered to the Khamis Mushait Air Base in the mountains of southwestern Saudi Arabia. Operation Desert Shield had begun.

On a warm June evening in the late 1970s, two Little League teams played a hard-fought game in suburban New Jersey. Naturally, both sides wanted to win, but the thin black pitcher was more intense than the other kids. Troy Gregory relished baseball as a chance to compete—not only against his peers but against the high standards he had set for himself.

That evening Troy's team lost by two runs. Walking to the parking lot with his mother, he could no longer control his disappointment. He nodded toward his teammates. "They didn't try hard enough," he said, tears running down his cheeks. "If they had, we would have won."

Trying hard became Troy Gregory's watchword. When his mother, an artist struggling as a single parent, was unable to cope, the boy went to live with his grandmother, Grace Moore. They moved to a tree-lined street in the suburbs of Richmond, Virginia. There, Mrs. Moore—an old-fashioned, religious woman raised on a Virginia farm—renewed her grandson's self-confidence.

"Set a goal," she told him. "And when you reach that goal, set another. That's how people get ahead in life."

Gregory followed her advice and did well in school and sports. "I'm going to make something of my life," he told his grandmother.

Wanting to go to college and needing some financial backing, Gregory joined the Marine Corps Reserve. As soon as he was sworn in, he mounted a "Semper Fi" bumper sticker on his car to tell the world he was a Marine and proud of it. Gregory was assigned to Hotel Battery, 3rd Battalion, 14th Marine Regiment, a tight-knit field artillery unit, and trained in fire-direction control.

By the fall of 1990, Gregory was engaged to Adrienne Ward, an accounting student at a local university, and she took him home to meet her family in rural Virginia. He was enthralled by the warm throng of brothers and sisters, aunts, uncles and cousins. The couple decided on a large spring wedding to include the whole family.

The Gulf War, however, changed all that. The call came a few days after Thanksgiving. Gregory would be activated on December 2; Hotel Battery would join the 1st Marine Division in the Saudi Arabian desert.

That night, Gregory spoke to his fiancée with quiet sadness. "I wish I didn't have to leave you," he whispered. Later, he assured her that, if there was fighting, the war would be over quickly. "Start thinking about your dress," he said. "Pick out the music you want for the church."

Early on the morning of August 31, 1987, Robert Ray Tyler was riding his motorcycle to his first day of classes at Texas A&M University. As he sped toward a curve, the cycle skidded on a gravel patch, and he lost control. He broke a leg and his collarbone, and had serious internal injuries.

Tyler's mother, Cissy, received word of the accident that morning. God, no, she thought. Not again. In 1979, her husband, James Willis Tyler, had been killed in a motorcycle accident.

Cissy Tyler brought her son home for a long, painful convalescence. Ray Tyler had inherited his father's self-confidence and zest for life. When he was able to walk without a cane, he no longer looked forward to years in college classrooms. He was eager to get out in the world.

Tyler's father, his uncle Robert and his mother's fiancé, Rey Ortiz, had all served in Vietnam. Ortiz and Tyler's uncle encouraged him to consider the military. "It's a good way to get your feet on the ground and figure out what you really want out of life," his uncle told him.

So Tyler joined the Army's Armored Cavalry scouts. The Cavalry drove the new Bradley Fighting Vehicle, a high-speed personnel carrier armed with a fast-firing 25-mm cannon and TOW missiles. On his enlistment form, Tyler disguised the extent of his injuries.

After training, he was assigned to the 4th Squadron, 7th U.S. Cavalry, based in Germany. Their mission was to scout for the 3rd Armored Division, one of the most powerful units in the Army.

Tyler became the driver of one of Alpha Troop's Bradley crews, commanded by Staff Sgt. Edward Deninger. One rainy fall afternoon on a field exercise, deep in the hilly forests near the Czech border, the crew was working on the Bradley, drenched and covered with mud. "You know what you guys look like?" a friend shouted. "A bunch of old alley cats."

"Hey," Tyler shouted back, "I like that." Soon afterward, he stenciled "Alleykats" on the side of their turret.

Ray Tyler planned to go home for Christmas 1990. He called his mother to assure her that his division would not be needed in the Middle East. Just before Thanksgiving, he called again.

"Things don't look good," he said. The outfit expected to receive orders to go to the Persian Gulf.

On January 16, 1991, Col. Lewis Harned led the 13th Evacuation Hospital from a Persian Gulf port to northern Saudi Arabia, where the unit deployed behind a wide sand-mound "berm." Then, on the night of February 23, they braced for heavy casualties. The ground war had begun.

The next day, American and Iraqi wounded poured into the unit's helicopter landing pads. Some of the casualties were beyond even the intervention of the 13th Evac. Miraculously, surgeons pulled other soldiers from the brink of death. During a howling sandstorm on February 28, one young American arrived in deep shock. His tank had taken a direct hit. One leg had been severed above the knee, and there were multiple open fractures on the other; his left forearm was shredded; his groin was ripped by shell fragments, and his right eye was shattered beyond repair. As one surgical team patched segments of his veins into the arteries of his fractured leg, another attended to the soldier's other wounds.

By four o'clock the next morning, the soldier was stable enough to be evacuated to a military hospital in Germany. But there was still one important act to perform.

Capt. Juan Flores woke Dr. Harned from a deep, exhausted sleep. Together they went to the brightly lit evacuation ward where the soldier lay strapped to a stretcher beneath heavy blankets.

As Captain Flores read a citation, Colonel Harned bent to pin a Purple Heart to the young man's pillow. Then Harned grasped the soldier's uninjured hand. "We are all extremely proud of you," he said.

Tears began streaming from the G.I.'s unbandaged eye, and Harned felt a hot salty sting on his own face. When he looked at the tired faces of the doctors, nurses and corpsmen who crowded around the stretcher, every one of them was crying too.

For Paula O'Connor, the war began on the afternoon of January 16. The deadline for the Iraqi withdrawal from Kuwait had passed and O'Connor joined the dayshift in the cavernous aircraft shelter as they armed two F-117As with laser-guided bombs.

Finally, the last fuse was tested, and the last bomb-bay door sealed. As the pilots climbed into their cockpits, O'Connor looked up at the captain perched above her. He stared back, his eyes impassive above the rim of his oxygen mask.

"Bring it back safe," she said into the crew chief's headset.

The pilot raised a gloved hand, thumbs up. "You bet," he answered. "See you tomorrow."

The aircraft rumbled onto the taxi ramp, and one by one they rose into the clear desert night. Soon their nose lights winked off. They were invisible.

Just before 3 a.m., a Stealth fighter from O'Connor's wing dropped the first bomb of the air war, destroying a radar station outside Baghdad. For the next 41 nights, the fighters of her unit flew more than 1200 sorties, bombing targets in Iraq and occupied Kuwait. O'Connor worked 12-, then 18-hour days, as the pace of operations increased. The crews grew closer than a family, each member watching out for the other, double-checking the work. It didn't matter that O'Connor was a woman. She was engaged in a vital combat assignment.

Ray Tyler and Alleykats led the 3rd Armored Division into Iraq on the afternoon of February 24. Engineers had cut wide lanes through the berms and mine fields along the border. From the open hatch of the driver's "hole," Tyler could see the dust columns of thousands of armored vehicles moving behind him.

For the next 48 hours, the division, screened by Tyler's cavalry scouts, plunged deep into Iraq across a hundred miles of desert. Tens, then hundreds of surrendering enemy troops swarmed out of bomb-blasted bunkers as the Bradleys fired on the fortifications.

By midday on the 26th, the division had reached its point to pivot east and assault the elite Republican Guard dug in along the northern Kuwaiti border. A howling sandstorm blew up, reducing visibility to 300 meters and forcing the gunners to rely on their thermal sights, normally used at night. The sights showed only ghostly, reddish hot spots, not the crisp detail of the optical instruments.

To the left of Alleykats, the crew of "3-6," its sister Bradley, commanded by Sgt. Ron Jones, scanned the sector ahead. Suddenly gunner Darren McLane spotted three wavering hot spots in his sight. "Bimps!" he shouted into his helmet mike, G.I. slang for Iraqi BMPs, armored personnel carriers.

In Alleykats' turret, gunner Clint Reiss sighted more BMPs at the same moment. "Light 'em up!" Ed Deninger ordered.

Reiss and McLane fired their cannon, and the thermal sights flashed with the glare of burning Iraqi vehicles. More BMPs appeared ahead among the sand dunes, firing at the advancing scouts. Down in the driver's seat, Ray Tyler had a clearer view than the men in the turret. What he saw frightened him.

Republican Guards were swarming along the ground, lugging rocket-propelled grenades and strange, suitcase-like missile boxes.

"Dismounts," Tyler yelled into his microphone, "eleven o'clock, a bunch of them."

Now larger, more ominous shapes appeared in the blowing sand ahead. The roar of heavy tank cannon sounded above the cracking of the Bradley's lighter weapons. Darren McLane rotated his turret and fired a steady burst of 25-mm rounds. Each round hit, but there was no explosion.

My God, McLane thought, *it's a T-72 tank!*

He switched to his missile control and fired a TOW. The explosion ripped the turret off the tank's hull.

Then, inevitably, the outnumbered scouts suffered losses. To the left, Sergeant Jones's Bradley took a hit from an enemy cannon round. The vehicle was now motionless, an obvious target.

"We're coming to pick you up," Ed Deninger called on the radio.

Ray Tyler raced to position Alleykats between 3-6 and the enemy, to shield Jones's crew as they bailed out. Platoon leader 2nd Lt. Michael Vassalotti had heard Jones's distress call as well. He raced his own Bradley up from the other angle and ordered Jones's crew inside.

Just as Darren McLane leaped from the top of the vehicle, 3-6's turret exploded. McLane was thrown to the sand and hit by shrapnel. His driver was also down. As Tyler watched frantically, the lieutenant's crewmen dragged the wounded inside.

"Get out of here," Deninger ordered. Just as Tyler pulled away, two T-72 sabot rounds hit Vassalotti's vehicle. Smoke poured from the holes, but incredibly the Bradley still rolled along.

Mortar and artillery rounds exploded now in the sand as the Iraqis fought desperately to disengage from the scouts of Alpha Troop. Deninger's order echoed in Tyler's ears as he went left, then right, then straight ahead. Finally, the platoon fell back to allow the heavy American armor forward in pursuit of the fleeing enemy. Four American vehicles had been destroyed or damaged, two men were dead, and 12 wounded. But that evening, as the troop formed into a circular defense position, their radios crackled with news that the 3rd Armored Division had overrun the fleeing tanks and BMPs, and was ripping the enemy apart. By God, Tyler thought, we did it.

Troy Gregory managed to call home one last time before his unit moved north to the Kuwaiti border. "Don't worry," he told his mother. His job, he explained, was to help select fire positions as the assault column advanced. He would be well back from the forward units.

In the predawn darkness of February 23, Gregory's battalion rumbled forward, a wedge of TOW-equipped vehicles and heavy trucks towing howitzers. The flat horizon lay hidden beneath a sooty pall of smoke from the hundreds of wellheads the Iraqis had set aflame in the Al Burgan oilfield.

For three hours on the 24th, the Marines repelled a savage counterattack by enemy forces. That night the troops dug in.

Along the horizon, the burning carcasses of Iraqi armor lit the overhanging smoke with flickering tongues of orange.

"Isn't this something else?" asked Cpl. Chris La Civita, a gunner in Hotel Battery. "It's like fighting in hell."

The next morning, as the Marines moved forward through dense, acrid fog, the Iraqis sprang a second, even larger counterattack. Enemy-tank rounds exploded in the sand, kicking up clouds of shrapnel. Several fragments hit Corporal La Civita in the face, ripping a bloody chunk of flesh from the side of his jaw.

As the counterattack threatened to envelop the battalion position, Gregory's survey team was ordered to search a nearby trench for enemy holdouts. As they entered a bomb-cratered bunker, Gregory tripped a mine.

An hour later, he was driven to the battalion aid station, where La Civita was waiting for the evacuation helicopter. Gregory was in shock, strapped to a stretcher, a medic holding a unit of blood plasma above him. But he was more concerned at the sight of his friend's heavily bandaged face.

"Man," Gregory whispered, "are you okay?"

La Civita's eyes filled with tears. One of Gregory's legs was blown off and the other was badly mangled. "Yeah, Troy," he said. "It's just a flesh wound."

"What about the other guys? I hope nobody else got hit when I stepped on that thing."

La Civita turned away to hide his tears. The battalion chaplain took Gregory's hand and prayed with him while corpsmen worked on his wounds. Finally the helicopter clattered down through the smoke to take the two wounded Marines to a field hospital in Saudi Arabia.

La Civita stayed with Gregory in the triage tent while corpsmen and nurses prepared the gravely wounded Marine for surgery. The next morning, La Civita searched for his friend among the patients. But Troy Gregory was gone.

Senior Airman Paula O'Connor returned to the quiet streets of Godfrey, Illinois, on a cool April morning. Her home was decorated with yellow ribbons, American flags and a huge "Welcome Home" banner. Her first request was for the Christmas dinner, with all the trimmings, that she had missed while on duty 7000 miles away.

After the initial excitement, O'Connor found herself spending quiet time with her dad. Dressed in jeans and a sweatshirt, she didn't seem much different from the tomboy who'd mastered a unicycle only 11 years before. But Joe O'Connor and his daughter found they had a new bond. Both had been to war.

Cpl. Robert Ray Tyler came home to McAllen, Texas, on a warm June afternoon. Cissy Tyler and her mother had prayed for his safe return for months. In their family, ties of love and devotion ran deep. But Tyler now felt a new kinship with his Uncle Robert and Rey Ortiz. Like them, he had gone to war when his country called.

On a breezy afternoon in late April, a chartered 747 jet landed at Bolk Field near Madison, Wisconsin. Almost a thousand friends and relatives lined the airstrip to greet the soldiers of the 13th Evacuation Hospital. Col. Lewis Harned was first out the door. His daughter Debbie's three young children rushed forward, each carrying a sign. Eric, four, held "Welcome." Catie, six, had "Home," and nine-year-old Jason, "Colonel Grandpa."

Harned, one of the oldest Americans to serve in the combat zone, grinned broadly. But his joy would always be tempered by the memory of the young Americans who had paid a heavy price to serve their country.

Lance Cpl. Troy Lorenzo Gregory, United States Marine Corps Reserve, was buried in Arlington National Cemetery on the raw afternoon of March 4, 1991. He had died two weeks before his 22nd birthday. His mother, grandmother and fiancée sat in the front rank of mourners while the Marine honor guard folded the flag that had covered the bronze coffin.

Beneath the collar of her funeral dress, Adrienne Ward wore the dogtag Gregory gave her before he left. Only now was she beginning to comprehend the scope of his sacrifice—and their lost dreams. She would never again see his warm smile, feel his loving touch. Then the March wind keened, as a lone bugler blew the somber notes of taps.

Over the next two weeks, the letters Gregory had written to his fiancée from his foxhole continued to arrive in Richmond. Reading his words, Adrienne Ward could almost pretend he was still alive.

Finally, one morning when the first buds of early spring appeared on the trees, the letters stopped.

THE WAR ON TERROR

★ ★ ★

One Man Bomb Squad

BY MARK BOAL
From *Playboy*

It's early December 2004 when a caravan of Humvees rumbles out of Camp Victory carrying Staff Sgt. Jeffrey S. Sarver's bomb squad from the U.S. Army's 788th Ordnance Company. Bouncing down rutted roads outside Baghdad, the convoy passes a helipad where Chinooks, Black Hawks and Apaches—some armed with laser-guided missiles and 30-mm cannons—thump in and out. Bradley and Abrams tanks sit in neat rows, like cars at a dealership, their depleted uranium bumpers precisely aligned. Impressive as it looks, all the lethal hardware is more or less useless against the Iraqi insurgency's main weapon in the war's current phase: the improvised explosive devices (IEDs) made from artillery shells, nine-volt batteries and electrical wire that now account for most American hostile deaths.

Turning onto a main road, the trucks enter Baghdad—massive, filthy, foul-smelling, and teeming with life despite two decades of war. Jumping curbs on side streets, the Humvees push through traffic like VIPs. The lead driver leans on his horn. In the .50-caliber machine gun turret up above, a gunner keeps his finger ready on the trigger. At last, the convoy arrives at an intersection. A Ranger team is manning a roadblock, and traffic is backing up.

Sarver darts out of his seat and up to a cluster of Ranger officers. He's just five-foot-eight in combat boots, and his helmet bobs near their shoulders as he steps up and slaps one of them on the back. "What's goin' on, boys?" he asks. "What have we got here? Where's the ah-ee-dee?"

The Rangers point to a white plastic bag fluttering in the breeze, 300 meters downrange.

Behind wraparound shades, Sarver, a baby-faced 33, considers the possibilities: Is it a real bomb or a decoy designed to lure him into the kill zone of a second IED? A hoax aimed at pulling him into a sniper's range? Is it wired to a mine? Daisy-chained to a series of other IEDs? Is it remote-controlled? On a mechanical timer or wired in a collapsible circuit that will trigger an explosion when he cuts it?

Sarver runs back to his truck, a few inches of belly fat moving under his uniform. He moves quickly, limiting his time on the ground. He tells Specialist Jonathan Williams and Sgt. Chris Millward to deploy the team's $150,000 Talon robot, with its tank-like treads and articulating plier grips. Using a laptop perched on the Humvee's hood, Millward starts up the bot. The Talon zips to the fluttering bag and pulls it apart.

But the job isn't done. The Army can't declare the area safe until a human explosive ordnance disposal (EOD) tech confirms with his own eyes that the bomb has been defused. It's time for Sarver to get into his bomb suit.

When Jeff Sarver was six years old, his dad, a carpenter, took him hunting for the first time. They left their home near Huntington, West Virginia, and went into the forest. His dad showed him how to be alone, how to be self-sufficient. He learned that if you were willing to bear the isolation of waiting for hours in a thicket, you could catch an animal in its natural grace, a flash of fur, muscle and hoof.

As he grew up, Sarver kept on hunting. He started with squirrels, rabbits and deer. One time, he shot a buck that ran 40 yards before dying. Later, he worked his way up to trapping coyotes and hunting turkeys. He fell for all of it. His mother never understood him. She always wanted to take him shopping, to visit relatives, or to socialize. He preferred to spend his free time hunting. When he wasn't hunting, he pored over hunting catalogs.

After high school, Sarver worked briefly as a carpenter before joining the Army at age 19. (He was following a family tradition: Both his father and grandfather had served in the military.) Once in, he proved himself an excellent soldier, a natural. After four years, he volunteered for EOD, where brains mattered more than biceps. He relished the challenge, and again, proved to be a natural.

Now, at the Baghdad intersection, Sarver's team kneel in the dirt, and, like squires attending a knight, adjust his armor.

Soon he is strapped into a 68-pound bomb protection envelope, a suit that, depending on the circumstances, could save his life from an IED blast.

"Come on, man, let's go," Sarver says as the men secure the suit. "Let's go."

Williams seals him in by inserting a clear visor over the helmet. He taps his boss on the shoulder, and Sarver is off, each step bringing him closer to the device. At 10 feet out, the point of no return, he gets the adrenaline surge he calls The Morbid Thrill. His heart thumps and his breath rasps over the amplified speakers in his helmet. "It's a numbing, sobering time," is how he describes it later. "It's the loneliest spot on earth."

Then he sees it up close, the IED, an ancient artillery round wired to a blasting cap, half-hidden in the plastic bag. Sarver grabs the cap and heads back toward the safety zone. He almost doesn't notice the second white bag sitting in a nearby gully. For a moment, he doesn't breathe. Should he run from this secondary bomb—placed specifically to kill him as he worked on the first one—or should he dive on it and take his chances? Deciding to act, he pitches himself into the dirt, reaching for the blasting cap with shaky hands. He pulls it apart, pink wire by pink wire (all the bombs here seem to be wired with the same discolored Soviet detonation cord).

Sarver exhales, removes his helmet and stands up. He is sweating, pale, and shaking from the rush. The area is reopened to traffic, and Sarver's Team One turns toward the base, speeding down Route Irish while mosques broadcast the call to evening prayer. Soon it will be dark, curfew time. The bomb makers will be at home. Sarver often wonders about these men. Would they shout *Allah akbar* ("God is great") if he were splattered on their streets?

As the Humvee rattles down the road, Sarver, lost in thought, stares out the window at the blazing Iraqi sunset. I like what I do, he thinks to himself.

Sarver arrived in Iraq from Fort McCoy in Wisconsin in July 2004. He was excited to be there. During his first nine years as an EOD tech, he'd been to Egypt, Bosnia and Korea, but those were peacetime jobs. This was a full-on combat operation. And with IEDs being the enemy's primary weapon, Iraq was the ultimate proving ground to a bomb tech like Sarver.

Not long after he arrived, he received orders to assemble a team and head to An Najaf, 100 miles south of Baghdad. When he and his team got there, the team joined up with the 11th Marine Expeditionary Unit. The Marines were fighting some 2,000 insurgents under the command of Shiite cleric Muqtada al-Sadr in the Wadi al Salam cemetery. (Among Shiite Islam's holiest places, the cemetery adjoins the shrine of Imam Ali, son-in-law of the Prophet Muhammad.) The insurgents fired on the advancing U.S. forces from behind gravestones and tombs. Little by little, American air power drove them back. But as they retreated, the insurgents booby-trapped the cemetery with mines, rockets and IEDs.

With the main U.S. fighting force backing them up, Sarver and Williams went in with a Marine EOD tech team. They worked together amid the tombs for the better part of two weeks, sweating like pigs in the 120-degree heat. Gaining 10 to 15 feet of ground at a time, they disarmed bombs as mortars crashed down around them. Sarver worked freestyle. He had to. There were no protocols to explain how to disarm a ground-to-air missile lashed to the top of a palm tree while dodging bullets.

When he wasn't being shot at, Sarver worried about the frag from the mortars exploding around him, scraps of metal traveling at 2,700 feet per second. More than that, he feared over-pressure, the wave of supercompressed gases that expands from the center of a blast. This compressed air comes at an unlucky bomb tech with a force equal to 700 tons per square inch and a speed of 13,000 miles an hour, a destructive storm that can rip through the suit, crush the lungs and liquefy the brain.

Once, toward the end of the month in An Najaf, Sarver and Williams were dismantling IEDs under heavy fire, and Williams began to shake, disoriented from the heat. Sarver sent him back to the Humvee for water. When Sarver himself returned to the truck, he found Williams prone in the back.

"Williams, where's the firing device?" Sarver asked.

"I left it back at the IEDs," Williams replied.

"Did you cut the wires?"

Williams stammered.

"Did you cut them? Did you cut them, Williams?"

"Yeah."

"Did you segregate them?"

"Yeah. But the mortars are getting really close."

"Did you put a charge on them?"

"No."

"Why didn't you put a charge on them?" Sarver yelled. Williams's health hardly mattered anymore. "Now we have to go back and blow them up."

As hair-raising as the incident was, Sarver never held it against Williams. Indeed, as they drove back to Baghdad, Sarver told the younger man there was no one he'd rather have at his back.

All army EOD techs get training in a school at Eglin Air Force Base in Florida. The Army looks for volunteers who are confident, forthright, comfortable under extreme pressure and emotionally stable. To get into the training program, a tech first needs a high score on the mechanical-aptitude portion of the armed-forces exam. One in four soldiers fail to graduate.

"We have not yet cracked the code on what makes a great EOD tech," says Sgt. Major Matthew Hughs, a senior officer at Eglin's bomb school. "The only way to find out if a man has the right qualities is to put him in the field, in the situation, and see how he does."

Right away, Sarver showed an intuitive grasp of engineering, even in training sessions. With a glance he could suss out any bomb's architecture. Later, when building practice bombs, he kept pace with his fellow techs, moving from shoe boxes with basic triggers to mock IEDs that incorporated motion detectors and multiple triggers linked by collapsible circuits.

To Sarver, EOD offered an infinite number of challenges—man-versus-materials moments when he would go down on a bomb and everything else fell away. He came to appreciate the fascinating and dangerous allure of each bomb, the beauty of a well-constructed killing machine. At times, he felt bomb work was better—far better—than hunting. In fact, there was only one problem with the job: There weren't that many bombs to disarm.

By September, Sarver's team was in Baghdad—6 million people spread over 81 square miles. It's a major urban center by any standard, with office towers and mosques, highways and traffic circles, middle-class neighborhoods like Mansur, and slums whose markets draw pedestrians by the thousands at midday. For the insurgents, the city is rife with platforms for killing Americans. Snipers wait for passing patrols atop tall buildings. Car bombers need merely pull up to a Humvee and wave hello before setting off a charge. In the slums, people bury IEDs in dirt roads amid garbage, in highway medians, even in the bodies of road kill.

The bombs come from a vast trove of explosives left behind by a dictatorship that spent wildly on weaponry. After one war with Iran, two with the United States and multiple Kurdish uprisings, Iraq's soil has become home to every imaginable weapons system, including an estimated 10 million land mines. Meanwhile, there are only about 150 trained Army EOD techs in Iraq. The Army plans to add up to 1,400 more in the next four years. One enticement: an extra $150 a month in "demolition pay."

In Baghdad, Sarver and Williams worked 48-hour shifts. The days blurred. Either it was morning or night; either you were driving out from the base or coming home; either the bomb was in a pile of garbage or in the carcass of a dead dog or on the side of the road; and either you disarmed it or you didn't and there were bodies or brains on the backseat of a truck.

It was hard to know how many bomb makers were in Baghdad. One expert said, "The skill set was spreading." Sarver read the intelligence reports he received closely, and tried to help by passing along bomb circuitry he collected on his missions. After coming back to base from a day in the field, he'd sort the bits of wiring he'd picked up on the Baghdad streets and place them in neatly labeled plastic bags. Later, they'd go to the FBI for analysis.

Like all EOD techs in Iraq, Sarver could trace the insurgency's history in devices he's disarmed. When he first landed, the bombs were rudimentary: a blasting cap, shell and command wire. Now they were more lethal, with wireless designs that incorporated modified car alarms, pagers and cell phones for remote detonation. Soon, he predicts, the insurgents will begin to use more advanced technology—which will push the death toll higher.

After every shift, Sarver returned to the base and painted a little bomb stencil on the door of his Humvee. One day, Staff Sgt. Kelsey Hendrickson, a tall, bald, strapping 26-year-old tech, watched as Sarver added another.

"How many you got now?" Hendrickson asked.

Sarver told him 120 IEDs and four vehicle-borne IEDs—car bombs.

Hendrickson lit a cigarette. "Who cares, anyway?" he said. "It's not like you get a special prize for disarming X number of IEDs."

"But I'll know," Sarver said.

By October 2004 Sarver and Williams have disarmed 160 IEDs. One day they are called out twice, but one IED goes off before they reach it, killing an Iraqi family driving by in a pickup truck.

Later, Sarver goes back to the trailer he shares with Williams. He's divided it with a wall of lockers. The only thing hanging on his wall: a map of Baghdad marked up to show places where bombs have been found, as well as areas where there's a good chance he'll encounter hostility if he's out on a call. He keeps pictures of his son, Jared, on his computer.

In December, with only a month left in their tour, the stress mounts for the bomb techs. Even under the best of conditions, EOD is a deadly job. Sarver knows it firsthand: A close friend, Staff Sgt. Michael Sutter, was killed by an IED the day after Christmas 2003, making him one of ten Army bomb techs to die in the field as of November 2005. And the chances of dying seem to surge in the last month of a tour, when fatigue, distraction and homesickness can dull a soldier's instincts. "You zig when the bomber zags," is how Sarver describes the kind of mental mistake that can prove fatal.

In the second week of December, in a rare instance when a colonel is in the field, Sarver's team travels to downtown Baghdad. They try to disarm the IED with a robot, but can't. Sarver must take the long walk by himself. Sgt. Chris Millward seals him into the bomb suit. Only Sarver's face, slightly distorted by his clear visor, is visible. If you look closely you can see him smile as he walks away. Beyond the smile, the rest of his face—the wide nose, small soft chin, and large blue-green eyes—is tight with terror.

As he approaches the bomb his mind goes blank: "Everything shuts down except for you and the device. I can hear myself breathing." His heart beats so loudly that it's audible in his helmet. Because the suit's radio receiver is turned off (to avoid sending stray radio waves that could set off the IED), Sarver walks toward the bomb totally cut off from his team.

"When you're 10 feet away from it," he says, "you get comfortable because you're at the point of no return." This particular bomb—a rusty metal cone—pokes out from beneath a pile of rotting garbage. Sarver puts his hands on the device, an artillery shell holding 18 pounds of explosives with a blasting cap cemented in the nose. A pink wire in the cap leads to a battery connected to a cell phone. A call to the phone opens a circuit that will send an electric charge to the blasting cap, which will detonate the entire contraption.

Sarver must separate the blasting cap from the main charge, but it won't come out of the cement. He grabs his knife and starts digging around the wire. He's careful not to upset the cap. It could blow from even a hard jolt. From 300 meters away, he seems to be moving at hyperspeed, but inside the bomb helmet the moments stretch out. It's like he's moving in super-slow motion. Finally, the wire gives. The bomb separates, and Sarver stands up.

After he finishes, the colonel, whose convoy the IED nearly destroyed, approaches. "Are you the wild man in the bomb suit?" the colonel asks.

"Yes, sir," Sarver says. "That was me."

"Look at that hero. America's finest," the colonel says, shaking Sarver's hand. "I want a picture with this man."

On Christmas Eve, with six days left in his field duties and 190 bombs painted on his truck, Sarver goes out to assess the damage caused by an oil-tanker-truck bomb that's gone off near the Moroccan embassy. When he arrives, the only light is from a fire smoldering in the top of a palm tree. The air, thick with debris, smells of sulfur, burned fuel and human blood.

Examining the site, Sarver shines his flashlight into the crater—9 feet long by 6 feet wide by 3 feet deep—left by the blast. He steps through the crunching glass and bits of metal to the truck's engine block and looks for traces of explosives. Army forensics experts and another EOD tech team are also on the scene. Among the questions to be answered: Was the bomb detonated remotely or the work of a suicide bomber?

Walking away from the center of the blast, Sarver follows the path of the destruction. At 40 paces, he walks through a completely blackened expanse, which gives way in another 5 paces to a few visible shapes—a bit of concrete, part of a wall. Then come recognizable things, charred but not consumed, and finally just singed—the blistered paint on a gate. Beyond that, weird-looking chickens peck at the dirt, their feathers burned off. Sarver aims his light up into the branches of a tree and finds an orange, perfect and ripe.

"This is where it ended," he says, then walks back to the center. He notices two well-dressed men standing in the doorway of their home.

"I'm sorry this had to happen to you," he says.

"I'm sorry too," says one of the men, a Kuwaiti.

"Was anybody hurt?"

"My brother, next door. The glass fell on him. But he's okay."

"I'm sorry. If you see anything hazardous, give us a call and we will come and take it away for you."

Back at base, the bomb techs tear into packages of Froot Loops, adding the bitter reconstituted Iraqi milk. They talk about cartoons and movie characters with funny-sounding names. Millward does impressions of Elmer Fudd and Daffy Duck. Williams laughs so hard that milk dribbles down his cheek. Sarver, ashen, leans against a wall. "The chickens are what got me," he says finally. "It was horrible the way they had their feathers burnt."

Before leaving Iraq, Sarver does a final tally of the bombs he's defused: 208. How many lives has he spared? Dozens, maybe, or hundreds. In his After Action Report, the commander of the 788th Ordnance Company, Capt. Christopher Wilson, notes that Sarver's team "rendered safe the largest number of IEDs that were disarmed by any one team since operations began in Iraq." As he sits on the military plane that will take him home, the Bronze Star he's been awarded is stowed away with the rest of his gear. Jeffrey Sarver is officially a hero.

At home in Wisconsin, Sarver returns to his modest rental. It's just as he left it. None of his 100 rifles, shotguns and handguns have been moved from their cabinets. The living room also looks fine, still crowded with animal mounts—a turkey, a fox, a beaver, a raccoon, a coyote and a deer. They're all positioned on the walls in such a way that he can admire their lush fur and feathers while sitting on his couch.

After a brief hunting trip, he's back to active duty. Except this is what his life is like now: filling out forms, answering to civilians, killing time. There's little need to put on the bomb suit—only once a month, maybe, to respond to a suspicious package. Then there's the occasional call from a family that's found a World War II pineapple grenade in their dead grandfather's trunk.

When a day off arrives, Sarver decides to visit his family. He drives to Ohio to spend several days with his father. Next, he travels to Michigan to visit his son, Jared, who lives with his mother, Sarver's ex-girlfriend. When the three of them meet at the hotel where Sarver is staying, there are hugs all around. The talk turns to Jared's upcoming birthday (he'll be eight), and Sarver agrees to take the boy shopping for an early birthday present: a go-cart. In the calm Michigan evening, there are no IEDs to defuse, no bombs to harm his son. Staff Sergeant Jeffrey S. Sarver is at home in the nation he has sworn to protect—and a long way from the loneliest spot on earth.

Mark Boal is an American journalist, screenwriter, and film producer. He won Academy Awards for Best Original Screenplay and Best Picture for The Hurt Locker. *His screenplay for* Zero Dark Thirty *was also nominated for an Academy Award.*

The Men He Left Behind

BY BRIAN MOCKENHAUPT

While his men patrolled the farmland of southern Afghanistan, Sgt. First Class Carlos Santos-Silva came home to his wife, who had bought a new blue sundress embroidered with pink flowers to greet him at the airport. They'd planned to celebrate their twelfth wedding anniversary in Washington, D.C., during his two weeks of leave from the war zone. They would tour the capital and visit some of Santos's men recovering from injuries at Walter Reed Army Medical Center. Instead, Kristen wore her new dress to Dover Air Force Base and watched six soldiers carry Santos off a plane in an aluminum box draped in the American flag. "We're here together," she told me the night before the funeral and their anniversary, April 12. "This just isn't how I thought it would be."

Outside the funeral home in Arlington, Virginia, she gathered with friends and family, and handed out balloons, 12 blue and 12 white, for each of their 12 years together. At the signal, the others released their balloons on cue, but Kristen wouldn't let go. She gazed skyward and her lips trembled. After a long moment, she opened her hand, and watched the balloons rise. "I love you, Carlos, forever and ever and ever," she said, then covered her face with her hands, and shook with sobs. Cameron, their 11-year-old son, stood next to her and pressed his face to her hip.

The next day, under a cloudless sky, she buried Santos, 32 years old, in Arlington National Cemetery. A horse-drawn caisson carried his casket down a road lined with tall shade trees to Section 60, where the headstones chart the histories of the Afghanistan and Iraq wars. Sgt. First Class Raul Davila stepped to the casket. He and I had both known Santos for years, having served two deployments with him in Iraq. Santos had gone on to become a drill sergeant, training new soldiers, and then a platoon sergeant with Charlie Company, 2-508th Parachute Infantry Regiment, 82nd Airborne Division, leading 40 men in the Arghandab River Valley, a violent swath of southern Afghanistan. Davila spoke about how Santos loved being a husband and a father and a leader of soldiers. "I will forever be honored to call him my friend," Sergeant Davila said, his voice steady and solemn. "Rest easy, Brother."

Gunshots cracked the warm morning air, a bugler played Taps, and in crisp movements practiced thousands of times, the burial detail pulled the flag tight and folded it into a neat triangle of stars on a field of blue. A general knelt beside Kristen and handed her the flag. I looked at the crowd, at those who had known Santos at so many points during his life. But what about those who weren't there, those who knew him best over the past seven months, those with him the day his truck rolled over a massive bomb buried in a dirt road snaking through farmers' fields? Santos's men were still working, in a lush, dangerous corridor of orchards and grape furrows outside Kandahar

City. As has happened thousands of times during the wars in Afghanistan and Iraq, when soldiers are killed and their bodies sent home, their friends stay behind, to mourn and remember and fight. I wanted to meet the men Santos had lived with and led. And for that, I'd have to go to them, to a place they called the Devil's Playground.

Flying into Afghanistan, I peered out the window at the vast stretches of brown, interrupted by jagged mountains, scored by rivers and dotted with villages. Down there, somewhere, Santos had been killed. At this height, such an explosion wouldn't even be visible. But staring at the land where he died and where his men were still fighting, his death seemed more real than it had at the funeral.

I would be staying with Santos's platoon at Combat Outpost (COP) Tynes along the edge of the Arghandab River Valley, northwest of Kandahar City, named for another lost soldier, Pfc. Marcus Tynes, who was killed November 22, 2009. To get there, I rode in the last truck of a five-vehicle convoy. We'd soon be passing over the very spot where Santos was killed, just beside a small bridge on a road where several bombs had exploded in the past six months. Looking through the windshield from the backseat, I watched a giant fountain of dirt shoot into the air 200 yards ahead. The concussion rattled my chest. "I.E.D.! I.E.D.! I.E.D.!" crackled over the radio, the same call made when Santos's truck was hit. An improvised explosive device planted in the same spot near the bridge had just exploded. But this time the insurgents were too hasty, the bomb went off too early, and the target truck rolled on, its crew uninjured.

After Santos's death, the region became even more dangerous. His men patrolled pomegranate orchards and vineyards where gunmen shot at them from the cover of dense foliage. The roads and trails were laced with buried bombs, making every step a life-or-death gamble, and the heat—100 degrees and humid—left them parched and exhausted. They had been ordered to begin "pacifying" a small stretch of the valley, so the Taliban couldn't use it to transport and store weapons and stage attacks on nearby Kandahar City. Their progress was hard to measure. For every bomb found, or fighter captured or killed, there were many more hiding in the valley. But the soldiers kept their fears in check and patrolled the orchards, doing it with a proficiency that would have made Santos proud.

At Combat Outpost Tynes, a former school, Santos's legacy was immediately apparent. When the platoon had moved into the compound in December 2009, soldiers slept in the few small classrooms, or outside, until Santos coordinated a construction project. The platoon then extended the structure and built small rooms for each soldier. During the slow, hard work of building up the rooms and the outpost's outer defenses, Santos had been beside his men, filling sandbags and lugging materials. "He was always hands-on with us," Staff Sgt. Edward Rosa, the platoon's senior squad leader, told me. "He was always out there with us working. He did everything with us. He was about the guys." He organized movie nights with a wide-screen television powered by a gun truck's battery. And at Christmas, after Kristen and the platoon's family support group sent stockings from Fort Bragg, he played Santa at the outpost. He made each man sit on his lap before he'd give him a stocking.

Santos was born in Germany to an Army family and bounced around bases as he grew up. He enlisted in 1996 and trained as a mechanic in an aviation unit at Fort Campbell, Kentucky, where he met Kristen, who was also in the Army. But he soon switched to the infantry, where he excelled. I served with him at Fort Drum, New York, for three years, and he impressed me as the most knowledgeable but laid-back soldier I knew. He could answer any question on tactics, weapon systems, or Army regulations, but he was also quick with wise-cracks and constantly concerned about his men. The soldiers at Combat Outpost Tynes told me the same. He played video games with them, gave professional guidance, and counseled them on problems at home. And he often made jokes when his men faced danger, to put them at ease and remind them that good could be found even during dark and fearful times.

"I heard stories about how tight people get when they deploy, but I never knew it could be like this," said Spc. Clayton "Doc" Taylor, the platoon's medic. "I called him Dad." So did many of his men. Sgt. Adam Lachance had never had a male friend like Santos. They had planned a couples trip to Las Vegas, and Santos and Kristen would visit Lachance and his wife in New Hampshire. Lachance had even turned down a promotion to staff sergeant in February because it would mean switching platoons and leaving Santos.

Each platoon is led by an officer, a first or second lieutenant. The platoon sergeant serves as his right-hand man in administration and logistics. That means Santos could have stayed behind at the outpost while his men patrolled. But he was always with them, as he was on the morning of March 22, in the front passenger seat of a hulking, mine-resistant truck, driving down a dirt road alongside a vineyard, just about to cross that small bridge.

Three miles away, Staff Sgt. Edwardo Loredo heard the call crackle over the radio as he led a foot patrol through the farmland south of the outpost. "Our guys just hit an I.E.D.," he said. Sound takes about 15 seconds to travel that far, so another moment passed before they heard the blast. Even at that distance, it rumbled through their chests. The bomb had been huge. The radio crackled again: "Four responsive. One unresponsive." Loredo's patrol ran toward the sound of the explosion.

Weighed down by 50 pounds of body armor, ammunition, water, radios, and weapons, they ran through farmland that may have been mined. Panting and sweating, leg muscles and lungs on fire, they arrived just as the medevac helicopter lifted off in a wave of dust that blocked out the sun. A tan armored truck lay on its side, the bottom scorched and the rear tires blown away, next to a deep crater in the dirt road. Sgt. Dale Knollinger, still out of breath, approached Sgt. Gregory Maher, who had been in the four-vehicle patrol.

"He's gone," Maher said.

"Who's gone?" Knollinger asked.

"Sergeant Santos."

Knollinger stood in the road and cried.

For a week afterward, Combat Outpost Tynes was quiet. "There was just silence for a while," Knollinger said. "There wasn't joking around like there was before." Soldiers talked to each other in quiet voices or kept to themselves. Santos's men felt adrift without him. "They lost their rudder," said Cpt. Jimmy Razuri, the commander of Charlie Company at the time.

Lachance had planned to bring Santos a McDonald's double cheeseburger from Kuwait on the way back from his two weeks of leave. Instead, while he sat in the Atlanta airport, his wife called with the news. Back at the outpost, he found soldiers in Santos's room packing everything to be sent home to Kristen. "I didn't know what to do with myself for a while," he said. He slept in silence. No more late night or early morning knocks on his wall from the adjacent room, Santos summoning him to hang out. He hadn't minded coming back to Afghanistan from leave, knowing he'd see Santos.

Now what? Lachance thought.

On his first patrol after his friend's death, Lachance reached into a pouch on his body armor and pulled out a handful of Jolly Rancher candy, the small pile speckled with green apple candies. His breath caught. He always carried Jolly Ranchers on patrol, and Santos took all the green ones, every time. "Why can't you just take a few?" Lachance would ask him. And Santos would just laugh.

Lachance stuffed the green candy back in the pouch. "I wouldn't touch them," he told me.

Several weeks before, Lachance, a self-trained tattoo artist, had given Santos a tattoo. The words snaked around his right arm: "The only thing necessary for the triumph of evil is for good men to do nothing." Beneath them, the date: 22 November, 2009, when Private First Class Tynes and another soldier in Charlie Company, Sgt. James Nolen, died. After Santos's death, ten platoon members asked Lachance for the same tattoo. One now wears the quote on his thigh, another on his bicep, another on his ribs, all followed by 22 March, 2010, and C.M.S., Santos's initials.

The platoon said goodbye to Santos at a memorial service at Combat Outpost Tynes several days after his death. His men filed up to the helmet resting atop a rifle propped between a pair of combat boots. They saluted and knelt and said silent prayers. And while they kept patrolling, they were rattled by the death. "If it happened to him, it could happen to any of us," said Staff Sgt. Edward Rosa, the platoon's senior squad leader. "That was the beginning of the craziness in the Arghandab for us."

In the coming weeks and months, the platoon was shot at and blown up repeatedly, sometimes several times a day. Spc. Brendan Neenan died June 7 in a blast that wounded four other soldiers. A buried bomb killed Loredo on June 24, and another bomb hit Spc. Christopher Moon on July 6. He died a week later at Landstuhl Regional Medical Center in Germany. Of the 42 platoon members, six were killed during the deployment and 14 injured, a casualty rate of nearly 50 percent, high even for frontline troops working in the country's most dangerous areas. By mid-July, the height of fighting season, many in the platoon were convinced their fate would be the same. But Moon's death was the last, and by mid-August, Santos's men had started boarding planes for home.

On September 11, 2010, I grilled chicken wings with Doc Taylor under a gray sky at a park on Fort Bragg in North Carolina. Country music blared from the open doors of his white Chevy pickup truck. Taylor's wife inflated a plastic palm tree as Kristen Santos opened a box of plastic Hawaiian leis. She and Santos had planned to throw a luau for the guys after the deployment. She figured he would have wanted her to follow through, and soldiers could share memories with her and the widows of Nolen and Loredo.

On a picnic table in an open-air pavilion, Kristen arranged framed photographs of the platoon's six dead soldiers on small stands and placed a yellow rose and a shot of Jack Daniel's in front of each. She held the large picture of Santos, standing against a gray concrete wall in Afghanistan, his rifle propped up beside him. "I miss him so much," she told me, and kissed the photo. "It still doesn't feel real."

Such distance from the battlefields where their loved ones died leaves many family members without a sense of closure. Kristen said it was difficult for Cameron to accept that his dad was gone. He had been away a lot. He'd been deployed over Halloween and Thanksgiving and Christmas. Now, the only difference was Cameron had been told that his dad would never be coming home. Kristen understood. She had last seen her husband on Thanksgiving Day, 2009, when they chatted by video for a few minutes during a rare moment of Internet access. She still couldn't quite believe she'd never see his face again. She welcomed his soldiers home when they stepped off the plane, hoping for some feeling of finality, which eluded her. "I went to all the flights just to prove to myself he wasn't coming home."

Soldiers wearing Hawaiian shirts arrived with wives, girlfriends and children, plates of food, and cases of beer. The pavilion filled up and Captain Razuri stood in front of the memorial table. "Nine years ago today, you know what happened," he told the group. "It's why we're still doing what we're doing today, and why these guys behind me aren't with us."

Later Kristen sat with a half dozen soldiers and looked through pictures from the deployment, many of which she hadn't seen. Santos walking through villages, filling sandbags at COP Tynes, drinking tea with the Afghan police, handing out stockings for Christmas. Kristen laughed and reached toward the laptop computer screen, as though to touch him. And then the pictures changed, from shots of a grinning Santos to soldiers standing on a dirt road, next to a truck flipped on its side, scorched by flame, two wheels blown off. The laughter stopped, and Knollinger and Rosa traded nervous glances with other soldiers. "I need to see this," Kristen told them. She leaned closer to the screen and stared at the pictures. "Is that the truck? I need to see where it happened. I need this."

Kristen and the soldiers told stories about Santos and, one by one, his men sat for a few moments and wrote on the big framed picture she had brought. By day's end, the border around the photo was crowded with messages to their fallen leader.

> *I want you to know you changed my life and I love you for that. The world will never be the same without you. But I will be the man I told you I would. I love you, Dad. Till we meet again.*
>
> *Doc Taylor*

Dad, I can't even describe what it was like to work for you. I learned so much and matured because of you. You were awesome to work for and truly a great friend. I love you and think about you every day. Miss you.

Sgt. Dale Knollinger

You were the quiet professional. Thank you so much for your guidance. You have no idea how much you are missed. Goodbye, Brother.

Sgt. Brian Flannery

I've never been closer to another man. You were a great friend. Until we meet again, you will be thought of every day.

Sgt. Adam Lachance

That night, after Kristen packed up the leftovers and pulled down the decorations, she and Cameron returned to their small brick house on Fort Bragg, crowded with pictures of her husband. Cameron retreated to his bedroom to play video games, as he had often done with his father and now did alone. Beside him on the bed lay the framed picture, adorned with the memories of the men his father left behind.

★ ★ ★

Miracle Mission

BY ANTHONY FLACCO
From *Tiny Dancer*

The green beret was on routine patrol in a busy marketplace in Kandahar when he spotted a man walking with a girl about nine years old. His daughter, probably, the soldier thought. On this morning in February 2002, in southern Afghanistan, the American might not have given the two of them a second thought. Then the scarf wrapped around the girl's head slipped off—giving him a glimpse of her hideously scarred face.

My God, what happened to her? the soldier wondered. Burn wounds covered her face, neck and chest, and she seemed wispy-thin even by the scrawny local standards. About 4 feet tall, she couldn't have weighed more than 60 pounds, the soldier thought. He'd never seen a child disfigured so.

Still, even in her condition, the girl was alert and seemed to sense him looking at her. She raised her eyes and stared directly back. Intrigued by her curiosity and defiance, the American approached the man and, speaking the Dari language a little and gesturing, asked him what had happened.

There'd been a fire at home, months before. The girl had escaped with her life, but now the scarring on her face and neck was threatening her ability to eat and even breathe. Her skin was either raw and fragile, or twisted with ugly welts. She could no longer close her mouth or eyes. The father had brought her to Kandahar, more than 200 miles from their desert home in Farah, to try to find medical help.

And what was being done for her? asked the soldier.

"Nothing," replied her father. The doctors weren't hopeful, he said.

Introducing himself as Mohammed Hasan and his daughter as Zubaida, the man said he had eight other children at home. He was a farmer, a peaceful Shiite Muslim, he said. He had sold most of his meager possessions and borrowed money from neighbors to pay for his long trips around the country to try to find help for his daughter. The soldier marveled: In a land that put a notoriously low value on females even in the 21st century, this struggling father had basically ransomed his life to try to help his little girl.

The American couldn't just walk off and leave this child to die. If you could look past her scars, he thought—and admittedly that was tough, even for a Green Beret—you could see a spark in her eyes. The soldier told them, "Come with me," and waved for them to follow.

Alone in her family's mud hut seven months earlier, it was easy for a girl of nine to lose track of details while preparing a bath—like making sure the pilot light was out before she filled the heater with kerosene. Zubaida, who loved music and dancing, had also neglected to kick her shoes out of the way before she sashayed toward the heater. She tripped and fell hard, just inches from the water heater, dropping the kerosene can.

A wave of fuel splashed over the heater's pilot light and directly onto Zubaida. A sheet of fire roared, igniting the fuel and basically turning the girl into a human torch. She screamed while trying to beat out the flames on her hair and skin. When she inhaled, superheated air scorched her throat and lungs. She whirled and flailed, beyond panic.

Next door at a neighbor's, Zubaida's mother, Bador, and her elder sister, Nacima, heard her screaming, and arrived just in time to see Zubaida collapse. "The water, quickly!" Bador screamed.

They grabbed the tub and dumped it over the girl. That killed the flames, and now her mother and sister could see Zubaida all too clearly. She was a crumpled heap of terror and pain. And unfortunately, she never lost consciousness.

There was no phone in the village, so Daud, Zubaida's 16-year-old brother, ran to find their father while Bador, Nacima and some neighbors drizzled water over her burned skin. After an hour of complete torture, shock began to settle in, and Zubaida lapsed into uncontrollable shaking.

The local clinic had no way to treat such extensive burns, and no painkillers, either. After watching his daughter suffer for several days, Zubaida's father, Mohammed, headed for Herat, the nearest city. While a neighbor drove an old car 120 miles over rutted dirt roads, Mohammed held Zubaida in the backseat as she shrieked. Bador prayed in the front seat. The desperate trip took nearly seven hours.

At the clinic, Mohammed Hasan pulled out a small bit of currency and pressed it into a doctor's hands. "Please save my little girl," he begged him.

With third-degree burns—and Zubaida was covered with them—the cure, or at least the start of the cure, was almost as painful as the fire. In order to avoid infection, the girl's charred skin had to be scraped and washed. Without any anesthesia, the doctors in this tiny outpost hospital had to peel away the blistered skin across Zubaida's neck, throat and arms. It was pure agony for her and everyone around her; afterward, the doctors applied a salve. Then they released her. There was nothing more they could do.

The lead doctor pulled Hasan aside. "The injuries are not survivable," he said. "Death will surely come in a week or so. Take her home and pray for the end to come quickly."

Hasan wouldn't hear of it. "Pray for her to be spared," he said.

And she was. Months passed, and scar tissue continued to grow. It began stretching and pulling on her facial features, giving her the look of a melted wax sculpture. Her left arm, burned more than the right, became stiff. As the scar tissue continued to replace the dead skin, it formed a sort of web, so that her arm fused to her chest. Most people in the developed world, where there is adequate care for burn wounds and nearly everything else, will never see anything like it.

Now, though, in Kandahar in February 2002, Hasan and Zubaida followed the American soldier as he led them toward a U.S. base.

The Green Beret—as a Special Forces member, he remains nameless—took his charges to the 96th Civil Affairs Battalion. This was irregular, to say the least: It was just about five months since September 11, 2001, and American bombers and cruise missiles were still pounding every mountain and shadow in Afghanistan, hunting for Osama bin Laden. Even here, back of the main battle lines, everyone worried about terrorist infiltration. But the soldier insisted, and a medic agreed to examine Zubaida. Even so, the potential for trouble was enormous.

By the time the day was over, father and daughter had been guaranteed enough medical help to address Zubaida's immediate infections. The treatment might require days or even weeks. Cautiously grateful, Hasan took Zubaida off to find lodgings nearby, promising to return shortly after.

Word of the girl began to spread. State Department officer Michael Gray, age 40 and with boyish good looks, was working for Gen. Tommy Franks, coordinating humanitarian relief into Afghanistan. Once he learned about Zubaida, he went to work weaving a lifeline of security clearances, visas and medical forms to help bring her to the United States for treatment.

Gray's younger sister, Rebecca, was married to surgeon Peter Grossman; Peter and his father, Richard, ran the Grossman Burn Center at Sherman Oaks Hospital, near Los Angeles. Gray knew Rebecca would not be able to resist getting involved in this case.

He picked up the phone and called his sister at home in California. "Hi, Rebecca," he said. "Are you sitting down?"

"No," she answered. "Actually I'm standing up. What's going on?"

Once he told her the story, Rebecca called her husband at work. "Hi, honey," she began. "You're not going to believe the burn case the State Department has brought Mike." Peter was intrigued, and once the devastating photos of Zubaida were e-mailed to him, his interest only grew. He began making arrangements as well.

Peter and Rebecca had no children, though kids were their desperate wish. With formidable energy, Rebecca approached the Children's Burn Foundation, a California organization that raises funds for needy cases. The foundation quickly agreed to cover $300,000 worth of the costs of Zubaida's early medical procedures.

On June 10, 2002, U.S. military physician Mike Smith, accompanied by a translator, flew with Zubaida and her father from Kabul to London via Dubai and on to Los Angeles. Afterward, they were driven to the Grossman Burn Center. When he first met Zubaida, Peter Grossman was heartened: In spite of her injuries she looked directly at him. She said "hello" in memorized English and stuck out her good arm to shake his hand. When he told her his name—"Dr. Peter"—she quietly repeated it and made the slightest switch of a smile. It was all her injured face would allow.

In the coming months, Peter's impressions came to match those of all the other soldiers and doctors who had met Zubaida along the way. To an able-bodied person, this child's endurance and will to live was humbling.

Early on June 14, Peter Grossman's team prepped Zubaida for her first surgery. "Everything is going to be good," Peter told her. Her anxious father huddled with the interpreter in the waiting room.

Peter had assembled a stellar team to assist him. They agreed that his father, Richard, would team up with Dr. Alexander Majidian to free Zubaida's left arm from her chest. Surgeon Brian Evans would work with Peter on the first efforts to cut back scar tissue from the face, neck and chest. Since Zubaida was so young and weak, and her surgery so extensive, pediatrician Matt Young stood by. Dr. Charles Neal had the daunting task of handling the anesthesia. "There was a lot more tension than normal," said Peter Grossman. "With Zubaida's disfigurement, her anatomical markers were skewed; her vital structures were buried under those scars."

A complication showed up right away: Charles Neal was unable to get a breathing tube down Zubaida's throat because of the way her head was bent downward, pulled by burn scars. Even using the camera in a fiberoptic endoscope to guide the tube didn't work; the contraction was too severe. With limited time before the sedation would begin to suppress Zubaida's respiration, the pressure was on. The team had just minutes to insert the tube.

As soon as Neal had her far enough under, Peter made an incision around the chin line to cut through the bands of tightened scar tissue that were binding the chin to the chest wall. He was stunned to find a carapace of scar tissue half an inch thick; it was more like hide than skin.

The first of Zubaida's amazing transformations had begun. As soon as the incision was made around the jaw line, her head tilted back into a normal position. Now Neal could slide the breathing tube down her airway and begin a standard gas anesthesia. During the next hour and a half, as he cut away masses of scar tissue, Peter saw a little girl emerge.

The team performed two of the most dramatic and challenging procedures at the beginning—the first to release Zubaida's head and neck from the chest, the second to release her left arm from the torso. And a near-magical element of modern medicine came into play. The large open wounds where the scar tissue had been were carefully sprayed with Tisseel Fibrin Sealant, a complex "glue" for human surgical needs. It sealed off tiny points of bleeding and let the wounds stabilize before skin grafts were applied. In Zubaida's case, with so little healthy skin available, every graft would need to take; the sealant gave Peter a head start.

Under the bright lights of the recovery room, Zubaida began to regain consciousness. She felt no pain, though she did have some nausea; she had the feeling of being tightly wrapped in soft blankets. As she told her father later, she was wondering, Where am I? What's going on? Who are these strange people who look like ghosts?

Then it hit her: This is the American hospital. The men are doctors. This is part of their magic. And my face and neck don't hurt anymore.

In the waiting room, Peter told Zubaida's father that the operation had gone well. She would be in the hospital for the next few days, he said, until she was strong enough for the second surgery. Then grafts from her own skin would be placed over the surgical wounds.

Peter explained that after that step, they would be able to remove Zubaida's bandages; the skin grafts, he hoped, would be safely in place. This would be a long process: There were still perhaps ten more surgeries to go.

Hasan nodded to Peter in gratitude. It's working, he thought. The Americans are keeping their word to help my daughter.

Two days later, Rebecca Grossman came to the hospital to see Zubaida. She'd worked zealously behind the scenes to help Peter make arrangements; she also knew a host family had been found to care for Zubaida between surgeries. The family spoke Farsi, which was close enough to Zubaida's native Dari to allow conversation. Swaddled in bandages, Zubaida talked to Rebecca through the interpreter. Her pain was minimal, she told the lady with the honey-blond hair. And she was happy that Dr. Peter kept his promise not to hurt her. Rebecca's gentle warmth made the girl feel comfortable.

For Zubaida's second surgery, Peter and his team delicately harvested grafts from her unburned skin. Here's where art met science: Peter had to look at each burn area carefully, visualizing just how the wound might look in a week, a month, a year, even ten years. How would the grafted skin move with Zubaida's body? How would it react as she grew?

He went into the OR knowing that every square centimeter of each graft was vital, both in the short run as a defense against infection and in the long run as an integrated part of her healed flesh.

The second-round work went according to plan. It was just six days after the first surgery, and now, with the new surgery, Zubaida had a good amount of grafting in place. Peter would be unwrapping the bandages to check on the skin's progress; this was also Mohammed Hasan's chance to see the early part of his daughter's transformation before he had to head home to Afghanistan to care for the rest of his family, who awaited him.

Hasan watched in astonishment as Zubaida's dressings were gently removed. He finally saw what Peter and his colleagues had accomplished. Zubaida sat on the table in front of him, shivering from the air on her skin. In some ways she still looked dreadful—bone-thin and sickly. But her face and neck were now completely free of that thick and twisted scar tissue.

Her face was recognizable; her left arm was free. To demonstrate, Peter gently took Zubaida's arm and extended it all the way to the side and back again.

Hasan blinked. His eyes welled with tears and his throat seized up. When Peter offered Zubaida a mirror and she looked too, her eyes popped in wonder. She gazed at her father and smiled.

Hasan put a hand over his heart. He hugged Peter and heaped thanks on him without waiting for the interpreter to translate. They did magic on her, after all. The results were astonishing. She looked all patched up, but that dreadful monster of scar tissue was gone. Meanwhile, Zubaida kept smiling even though it hurt her to move her stitched-up features.

The next day Hasan kissed his daughter goodbye and returned to the airport. Within a few days, Zubaida was taken to her host family's home in nearby Encino for three weeks of recuperation. She still had at least eight more surgeries to go. In all, she was expected to be in America for about a year.

Zubaida's "foster" mother was of Afghan heritage, which was comforting. But Zubaida, still such a young girl, missed her father intensely. Her face-to-face confrontation with American life had been suspended while she was in the hospital; now she was bombarded with heavily accented language, new surroundings, strangers who smiled but who barely seemed real to her. As the summer days of 2002 drifted by, Zubaida experienced mood swings and emotional outbursts that reflected all her frustration and isolation. Nightmares made her cry out in torment. Everyone struggled.

On July 3, she had her third surgery, with Peter working on her skin like a custom tailor building a full-body suit out of living fabric. Permanent grafts were taken from healthy parts of her body and blended into the surrounding skin; as time went on, they would grow with the rest of her and not betray her by going out of control like the scar tissue had earlier.

Rebecca Grossman, meanwhile, found herself drawn to Zubaida in ways she never had been with any burn center patient. Feeling the girl's will as well as her playful spirit, Rebecca talked with Peter and with the host family. They arranged for Zubaida to spend a weekend, just the three of them, at their home in Hidden Hills. They had dogs, horses, a pool, and lots of time to share.

The visit went well—Zubaida arrived, smiling, carrying a little tote bag, and her mood stayed bright the entire time—and Peter and Rebecca began reveling in their brief role as surrogate parents. The house had a full feeling when Zubaida was around. As her healing progressed, the Grossmans took her on outings—bowling, to the beach.

Inside a Malibu cove, still careful of her condition, Zubaida played in the waves that broke on the sand. Peter and Rebecca watched as she came back to life, jumping around in the water like any other kid. It was like seeing an entire chunk of her healing process in a single afternoon. The day came, in November of that year, that Zubaida moved in with the Grossmans for the remainder of her time in America.

Not that things were perfect: So much had changed for Zubaida so fast. That first day at the Grossmans' home, she made her way into the kitchen and curled up into the safe, cave-like space under the kitchen table.

With the Grossmans' help, though, she was soon speaking to her father on the phone. She told him that Rebecca was enrolling her in public school while she was here. Hasan shouted with joy. "Soak up everything you can!" he said. "This is an opportunity no one here can even imagine." In her homeland, Zubaida had never once attended school. Now she was determined to learn to speak English and to read and write Dari.

That fall, as she continued to heal, she entered the third-grade class at Round Meadow Elementary in Hidden Hills. Teacher Kerrie Benson asked her class to try to imagine being far, far away from everyone they had ever known, without family or friends. "We need to do more than just help her learn things," she told the children. "We need to be like her family and friends, because that's what we would want others to do for us."

Though Zubaida was very timid, on her first day the kids argued over who would get to spend time with her. In spite of her poor English, she communicated well enough that she was soon fully enmeshed in classroom life, as well as the girls' social group after school.

Then came the holiday season—and the day Zubaida switched from calling Peter by his first name to calling him Dad. Little hairs stood up at the base of his neck as a smile made its way across his face. He watched Zubaida for a change of expression, some acknowledgment that she knew what she'd said. Instead, she just went right on chattering away.

She seemed to do best, he realized, when she could sort things out at her own pace. And he appreciated that the shift in her name for him revealed a deepening of her personal trust—far beyond the medical trust she had placed in him from the start.

Most Valuable Player

BY W. HODDING CARTER

Greg Gadson, a lieutenant colonel in the Army's Warrior Transition Brigade, is a natural leader—the kind of guy you'd be looking for on the battlefield. He's also the kind of guy Mike Sullivan, wide receivers coach for the New York Giants, thought could make a difference to his losing football team.

The two men had gone to West Point together but hadn't been in touch much afterward, until Sullivan walked into Gadson's hospital room at Walter Reed Army Medical Center, outside Washington, D.C., last June. Friends had told Sullivan that his former Army football teammate had suffered serious injuries in Iraq—resulting in both of Gadson's legs being amputated above the knee.

"This man had suffered so much," Sullivan recalls, "yet he was so happy to see me." The coach, who brought his old friend a signed Giants jersey with the number 98 on it, watched as Gadson interacted with the other patients and the doctors and nurses, encouraging them all. "To see the impact he had on these people—the look in his eyes and how they responded—was overwhelming and inspirational."

Sullivan couldn't help but be impressed by Gadson's enthusiasm and lack of self-pity. "He was bragging about me and talking about the Giants, and I was like, 'Hell, I want to talk about you. How are you doing?'"

When the Giants were scheduled to play the Redskins in Washington three months later, Sullivan sent his friend tickets—along with a request: Would Gadson speak to the team before they took the field? Having lost the first two games of the season, the Giants had already given up 80 points and, worse, seemed to be playing with no heart. The coach felt that Gadson was the perfect person to tell the players something they needed to hear about commitment, about perseverance, about teamwork. "A lot of the guys were frustrated and searching for answers," Sullivan says. "And I thought, This is someone who knows about pressure and sacrifice when it's life and death, not just a game."

Teamwork was everything to Gadson. He had played football at Indian River High School in the Tidewater region of Virginia and gone on to become a starting linebacker—No. 98—for West Point from 1986 to 1988, despite his relatively slight build of 190 pounds on a 5-foot-11 frame.

Following his graduation, Gadson, the son of a hospital pharmacist and a teacher, planned to serve his compulsory five years and get out. But after tours in the Balkans and Afghanistan, he found himself hooked. "Serving my country is important," he says, "but for me it's about being a soldier, being there for each other in the biggest sense of the word. I love being part of that team."

Last May, in Baghdad, Gadson was returning from memorial

services for two soldiers from his battalion when a bomb tore apart the truck he was riding in, knocking him clear of the vehicle and leaving him on the side of the road, bleeding and slipping in and out of consciousness.

He awoke ten days later at Walter Reed; a week later, after complications, his left leg was amputated, then his right. "I knew what had to be done even before the doctors told me," he says.

The night before the Redskins game, Gadson spoke with no script, from his heart. "You have an obligation not only to your employer but to each other to do your best," he told the Giants. "You're playing for each other. When you find a way to do things greater than you thought you could, something you couldn't do as an individual, a bond is formed that will last forever."

He told the team how much it had meant to him when his friends from West Point rallied around him in the hospital, and reminded them how powerful a team really is and how much stronger adversity would make them. "It's not about what happens to you in life," he said. "It's about what you do about it. It's about making the most of all your opportunities because I'm here to tell you, it can end in a flash."

When he finished speaking, the room was silent. "You could hear a pin drop," Sullivan says. And then it erupted in a standing ovation.

"You see a guy go through the things that he has, and he's in such good spirits," says Giants wide receiver Plaxico Burress. "I've never met somebody like that. I was like, Wow, I have a little ankle injury. I have to go out there and give it my best."

The Giants invited Gadson to watch the game from the sidelines the next day. When Burress scored the winning touchdown, he ran to Gadson and placed the ball in his lap. "All I thought about when I made that touchdown was that I wanted to find him and give him that football," Burress says.

The Giants went on to win their next ten road games. Gadson joined up with the team at the playoffs in Tampa, and again, they won.

Later, at the NFC championship game against Green Bay, the honorary co-captain sat on the sidelines in the subzero weather instead of in the heated box seat reserved for him. This time, it was Corey Webster who gave Gadson a football, after intercepting a pass from star Packers quarterback Brett Favre near the end of the game. The Giants won in overtime, 23–20, and the ball wound up becoming a piece of history. It turned out to be the last NFL pass Favre threw; he announced his retirement in March.

The Super Bowl was next, and the team flew Gadson, his wife, Kim, and their two children—Gabriella, 15, and Jaelen, 14—to Phoenix for the game against the New England Patriots, who'd had an undefeated season and were widely favored to win. The night before the contest, Gadson again addressed the players. And for the crowning touch on what became a legendary season, the Giants won, 17–14, their first Super Bowl victory in more than a decade.

"He is a powerful man with a powerful spirit," says Giants head coach Tom Coughlin. "And that is really what he gave us: the idea that the spirit rises above all these adverse conditions."

Physically, Gadson is making remarkable progress. He spends four hours a day in rehab, learning, among other things, to use prosthetic legs equipped with Bluetooth technology. Computer chips in each leg send signals to motors in Gadson's artificial joints so his knees and ankles move in a coordinated fashion. He is one of only two double amputees to use this technology, which was designed for single amputees. He uses a wheelchair or two canes most of the time but can also walk without support for short distances.

His family helps him remain upbeat. "I take great inspiration from my wife and kids," he says. "I don't always feel good, but I owe it to them to keep on trying."

Gadson isn't sure whether his role with the Giants will continue next season. He hasn't been discharged from the military, and his only official duty is to focus on his rehab. The soldier says he'd like to be there when his battalion comes home.

"I'm living the journey right now," Gadson says, reflecting on all that's happened to him in the past year. "I've come a long way, and I still have a long way to go. I don't believe you ever really arrive in life. You live life." And who knows where that will take you? If you are Lt. Col. Greg Gadson, you could go from the battlefields of Iraq all the way to the Super Bowl alongside the New York Giants—in a wheelchair, but never, ever sidelined.

Credits and Acknowledgments

"Unforgettable Eddie Rickenbacker," by Lowell Thomas, *Reader's Digest*, December 1973.

The Invasion: "The Great Decision," by Allan A. Michie; "Armada in Action," by Frederic Sondern, Jr.; "Beachhead Panorama," by Ira Wolfert; *Reader's Digest*, August 1944.

"Sergeant Erwin and The Blazing Bomb," by Corey Ford, *Reader's Digest*, July 1965.

"No Medals for Joe," by Mayo Simon, *Reader's Digest*, December 1990.

"Hero Of Sugar Loaf Hill," by Malcolm McConnell, *Reader's Digest*, December 1998.

"On a Wing and a Prayer," by Laura Elliot. Copyright © 1992 by *Washingtonian* Magazine (December 1992); *Reader's Digest*, April 1993.

"Those Navy Boys Changed My Life," by Carl T. Rowan, *Reader's Digest*, January 1958.

"1000 Men and a Baby," by Lawrence Elliot, *Reader's Digest*, December 1994.

"Veterans of a Forgotten Victory," by Ralph Kinney Bennett, *Reader's Digest*, July 1990.

"The Long Way Home," by John G. Hubbell, *Reader's Digest*, April 1952.

"The Courage of Sam Bird," by B. T. Collins, *Reader's Digest*, May 1989.

"Submarines to the Rescue!," by Ralph Seeley and Allen Rankin, *Reader's Digest*, December 1973.

"Beyond the Call of Duty in Vietnam," by Kenneth Y. Tomlinson, *Reader's Digest*, June 1970.

"A Hero Comes Home," by Kenneth O. Gilmore, *Reader's Digest*, November 1965.

"Pilot Down: The Rescue of Scott O'Grady," by Malcolm McConnell, *Reader's Digest*, November 1995.

"They Went to War," by Malcolm McConnell, *Reader's Digest*, September 1991.

"One Man Bomb Squad," by Mark Boal, copyright © 2005 by Mark Boal. *Playboy* (September 2005); *Reader's Digest*, January 2006.

"The Men He Left Behind," by Brian Mockenhaupt, *Reader's Digest*, March 2011.

"Miracle Mission," by Anthony Flacco. From *Tiny Dancer*, copyright © 2005 by Anthony Flacco; *Reader's Digest*, August 2005.

"Most Valuable Player," by W. Hodding Carter, *Reader's Digest*, May 2008.

Also Available from Reader's Digest